Tiger Salamanders As Pets

The Tiger Salamander Pet Owner Guide

Tiger Salamander Pros and Cons, Care, Habitat, Diet and Health all included

by

Eddie Silverthorne

DISCLAIMER

This book is intended for information and educational purposes only. While every attempt has been made to verify the facts and information provided herein, neither the author nor publisher assumes any responsibility for errors, inaccuracies or omissions, and specifically disclaim any implied warranties or merchantability or fitness for any particular purpose and shall in no event be liable for any loss of profit or any other commercial damage, including but not limited to special, incidental, consequential, or other damages.

In addition, neither the author nor publisher makes any guarantees, including but not limited to any express or implied endorsement of any the organizations, sites or other references listed in this book as resources for further information, assistance, equipment, or other uses. And the reader expressly assumes all risk in dealing with these sources. Furthermore, while accurate at the time of original publication, due to the ever changing nature of the internet and the world we live in addresses, links, urls, phones numbers and/or individual contact persons may not have changed.

Any slights of people or organizations are unintentional.

This book was printed in the UK and USA.

COPYRIGHT

ISBN 978-0-9926048-6-8

PIB Publishing
Pencross View
Hemyock
Cullompton
Devon. EX15 3XH
United Kingdom

Dedication

To all the lovers of those forever smiling Tiger Salamanders

Table of Contents

Chapter One: Introduction

The idea of domesticating animals is not new; we have been creating a chain of connections with animals in order to co-exist peacefully since the dawn of civilization. While history taught us to breed cattle, horses and poultry for personal consumption and profit, our relationship with the animal kingdom today has become more complex, even emotional.

We now view animals, not only as a source of profit, but also as a source of love and companionship. Through our discovery of new species and their natures, we have also changed the concept of domestication, with unusual animals being brought home with as much enthusiasm as the conventional ones. What is fascinating, however, is that people tend to have varied preferences when asked to select an animal they would like to house.

For some people, the perfect animal companion is one that is energetic, affectionate and boisterous. Those with a quiet demeanour may prefer an animal that is well-behaved, disciplined and calm. Some may describe their perfect companions to be those who swim behind large glass enclosures, providing tranquillity and beauty. And some others still may choose to bring home those pets that can be trained and raised for long-term profits. If you belong to that elite group of people who likes their pets to have a quiet unassuming demeanour and friendly attitude, Tiger salamanders may be the pets you've been looking for!

While the general family of salamanders has not been very popular as a pet to bring home and love, the Tiger salamander family enjoys the privileged position of being one of the most beloved pets in the North American continent. This is not surprising; one look at their beautiful striking bodies and permanently "smiling" faces is enough to melt anyone's heart! More than their appearance, however, it is their personality and character that wins them such high favour with pet owners.

Docile and shy by nature, these members of the mole salamander family prefer to spend their existence in quiet isolation, burrowing underground. Do not mistake their shyness for a delicate nature; these amphibians are also hardy and robust, and can adapt to a diverse array of environments and habitats. And despite their shy nature, these smiling creatures are also highly curious, making them among the more interactive members of their family.
A quality that makes the Tiger Salamander a prized pet is its ability to accept, even thrive in captivity. Provided it has the right conditions that include an optimum temperature scale, plenty of food and enough space to dig and retreat into privacy, your Tiger Salamander will live a content existence for up to 25 years.

These carnivorous creatures have generous appetites and a virtually unquenchable appetite. They are, however, also among the best-behaved amphibians, with rare signs of aggression, eccentricity or bouts of temper. They also adapt fairly quickly to human interactions, turning from shy housemates to smiling, even eager pets in a matter of days. Furthermore, these mild-mannered amphibians are of robust health as well, rarely succumbing, if ever not life-threatening diseases and illnesses. Their health and well-being is largely reliant on the kind of living environment you can provide. While breeding these majestic creatures is still a challenge in captivity, a single pet or a small group acquired from the wild or pet store will make perfectly healthy long-term companions, rarely arousing a need in you to breed more of them. It is no wonder, then, that Tiger

Salamanders are enthusiastically given a home by anyone who is lucky to encounter one of these.

If you, too, wish to bring home a Tiger Salamander, through this book, you will gain deeper insight in to its world - from its natural settings, to its behavioural patterns. You will also be guided through every stage of owning a Tiger Salamander, from initial thought to eventual raising. With a positive attitude and a dedicated spirit, you can work past the challenges that come with housing a Tiger Salamander and integrate them seamlessly into your life.

Chapter Two: Facts about the Tiger Salamander

The Tiger Salamander (Ambystoma Tigrinum) is a member of the mole salamander family and a species of salamanders unlike their cousins, in traits as well as behaviour with a lifespan of around 15 years, and living over even 20 years in captivity, Tiger Salamanders make for hardy and robust survivalists not only in the wild, but also as pets.

Tiger Salamanders are often mistaken for other lizards, and mistakenly classified as reptile. They are however, amphibians who exists both as aquatic and land-breathing animals, belonging to the mole salamander "Ambystomatidae" family of the caudate order. This makes them creatures who enjoy a preference of the quieter hours of the night to the daytime. Tiger Salamander, as members of the mole salamander family, also spends their days burrowing under the earth for spots to hide away from the rest of the wild. These spots also serve as spots during the winter months of estivation. After this stage of hibernation, the caudates emerge for breeding and mating.

Tiger salamanders are generally also known as Eastern Tiger Salamanders. Another closely related family of subspecies, the California Tiger Salamander, along with the barred Tiger Salamander (Ambystoma Mavortium) are sometimes classified as being part of the Tiger Salamander family, and are sometimes considered a different set of sub-species. This grey area in isolating their exact classification stems from the slight difference the caudates share in their physical anatomy and behavioural patterns. While most Eastern Tiger Salamanders, for example breed only through the monsoon months, the California Tiger Salamander, a type of Western Tiger Salamander, is known to breed throughout the year.

Furthermore, classification of the Tiger Salamanders as being either Eastern or Western was usually determined by the natural range of the species. In recent times, however, especially due to the demanding nature of scouting mudpuppies and larvae as bait in the fishing trade, several Tiger Salamanders have found themselves shipped across the country. In these new habitats, Eastern and Western Tiger Salamanders have mated and given rise to other subspecies, further blurring the line between the specimens. The most commonly found types of Tiger Salamanders in the wild today include tiger salamanders of the Barred, Blotched, Eastern, California, Mexico, Arizona and Spotted variety.

1. Physical Traits and General Appearance

The Tiger Salamander or Ambystoma Tigrinum, is an amphibian with four legs, a long tail and a distinct love for burrowing. Growing to a length measuring between 6 and 13 inches as adults, these shy and withdrawing caudate rely heavily on their physical appearance as a means of thriving, surviving and adapting.

As members of the mole salamander family, Tiger Salamanders are easily distinguished by their strong legs, even if they may extend from their bodies at peculiar angles. These legs are made suitable for burrowing activities with webbed feet that end in individual digits. The bodies themselves are stocky and sturdily built; to further the process of excavating earth for hibernating spots.

Tiger Salamanders are also known to have particularly pleasing faces on their broadly-shaped heads, with tiny protruding wide-spaced eyes, a wide and rounded snout and a sticky tongue that may poke out from a mouth curved into a perpetual smile. These facial features, in essence, are adapted for survival; the eyes perfectly shaped to withstand and encourage borrowing, the snout a tool for shifting small mounds of dirt, and the mouth designed to clamp down firmly on prey. When teamed together on a beautiful creature, these features give the caudate a look of permanent satisfaction, even slight amusement.

If you tried to go about poking a Tiger Salamander's head for ears, then you'd be sorely disappointed. Tiger Salamanders are known to make little or no sound, owing to the absence of vocal chords in their anatomy. What they also lack, are external ears or even eardrums. While this may deem the amphibians "deaf", Tiger Salamanders have actually been studied to respond to a different set of audio patterns. While research is still underway to confirm the details of this, Tiger Salamanders are believed to "hear" the sounds in their environment with the help of vibrations that echo when created between their feet, the floor and their immediate surroundings.

Completing their bodies is a long, tapering tail, with colorations and markings similar to those on the rest of the Tiger Salamander's torso. If you were to pay close attention to the upper surface of the tip of its tail, you'll notice a small granular areas housing a poison gland. This gland is meant to serve as an added defence mechanism that is expelled when the Tiger Salamander means to make a quick escape from its predator's clutches. It is worth noting, however, that the caudate will rarely use this poison gland as a means of self-protection, and even if released, is not toxic or deadly to humans.

And then we have perhaps the most captivating feature of the Tiger Salamander, its strikingly patterned skin. An easy misconception harboured by many people is that the Tiger Salamander's skin is similar to touch to that of a reptile's, such as a snake. However, a simple feel, even close look at the caudate skin will reveal that their textures and appearances are distinctly different. Tiger Salamanders have smooth, glossy, taut and well-hydrated skin that is without scales.

More than the feel of the skin, however, it is the coloration of the Tiger Salamander that attracts the human eye – while simultaneously warning away animals. Tiger Salamanders are found in a variety of subspecies with different coloration patterns and markings. Depending on the specimen available in your area, you will spot a Tiger Salamander by skin that falls in the colour spectrum ranging from black, to a pale olive, to a brighter green and even yellow. These shades are further highlighted by blots, patches or vertical stripes in a contrasting colour, the last pattern lending the "Tiger" label to this variety of mole salamander.

Therefore, you may spot a Tiger Salamander with dark blotches or stripes on a lighter background such as olive, or spot one with lighter blotches or stripes in colours like yellow, resting against a dark green, brown or black base colour. A broad colour palette means that this caudate can also be found in such unusual combinations as cream-colored or yellow stripes on a blue background to blue-grey backgrounds with orange markings. Flip the Tiger Salamander over, and you will find further displays of coloration -a yellow underbelly with dark patterned-markings or vice-versa.

As is inevitable with species that have distinct patterns of coloration which rely on pigmentation and other such factors, Tiger Salamanders, too, can have an "albino" appearance. The effect of irregularities in genetic chromosomal structure, albino Tiger Salamanders do exist, but are few in number and have very rarely been spotted.
These bright markings and colour patterns are used by Tiger Salamanders mostly as a sign of warning to ward off looming predators. To humans, however, their vibrant coloration, in addition to their seemingly happy faces and easy going natures, only makes them all the more desirable as pets.

2. Tiger Salamanders – Hatchlings and Larvae

When the breeding season rolls around, Tiger Salamanders usually make their way to a common breeding zone in the vicinity. Tiger Salamander babies are hatched in water, and their physical attributes as young ones are developed to thrive in an aquatic environment.

Yinug hatchlings and larvae have as little in common with the adults by way of appearance. With virtually no sign of initial colouring, Tiger Salamander larvae are tiny, with translucent, almost transparent bodies. As the initial stages of their development require them to swim more than burrow, larvae have no legs; in fact, the quirkily-shaped appendages only develop as the young ones approach the crucial stage of metamorphosis. Once they do begin their transition from larvae to adult Tiger Salamanders, however, the appearance and development of their useful limbs is a rapid process.

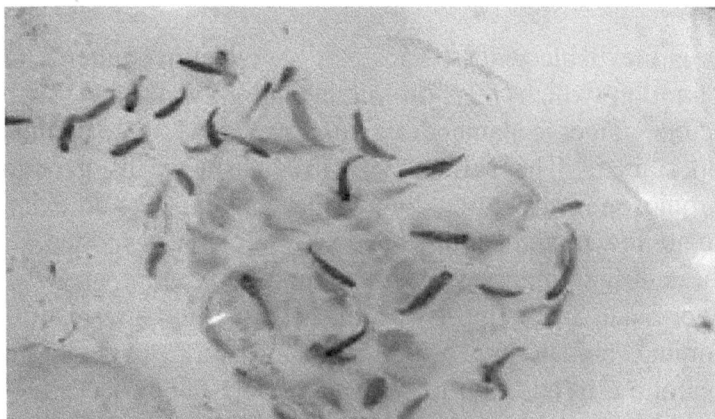

To enable comfortable breathing in water, Tiger Salamander larvae possess gills that protrude externally from their heads. These gills extend from the caudate body in long, feather-like tendrils, drawing out oxygen from the aquatic surroundings and passing it on to the larvae.

Around 4 to 4.5 inches in length as larval, Tiger Salamanders grow in length around the time of metamorphosis. This eventful period of transition from water-breathing to land-breathing amphibian does away with the external gills, make colourings and patterns more pronounced and ushers the larvae into adulthood and sexual maturity. While this process is known to take a little over two months, the period of metamorphosis itself varies between each subspecies, owing to a number of factors.

Areas that develop small water bodies, such as makeshift ponds or water catchments in the rainy seasons, or have water bodies that freeze in winters and are usable only in summers, become a popular breeding spot for Tiger Salamanders stranded with no permanent breeding pools. In such bodies, also called seasonal pools, Tiger Salamander larvae have been studied to undergo metamorphosis in alarmingly short periods of time. Such early-bird morphs are also labelled Small Morph Adults.

Conversely, those areas with warmer climates, permanent and abundant water bodies and even ancestral pools witness a longer period of transition from aquatic to terrestrial among the Tiger Salamander larvae. These young ones, in fact, have shown a tendency to metamorphose once they attain complete adulthood.

And then there those Tiger Salamander larvae who become so acclimatized with their aquatic surroundings, that they do not undergo metamorphosis at all. Instead, these aquatic Tiger Salamander adults, also known as neotenes, prefer to retain their larval breathing appendages and attain sexual maturity while still in the aquatic form. Neotenes are known to exist in those areas that do not harbour strong terrestrial conditions, essential for the Tiger Salamander's adult survival.

While Tiger Salamander larvae will need to undergo a cathartic period of transition to look like their adult versions, as young ones they bear a striking resemblance to another aquatic salamander known as the Mudpuppy. Almost similar to Tiger Salamanders in many aspects, Mudpuppies differ from the former in their inability to make a terrestrial transition. Remaining aquatic for life, Mudpuppies are a common source of fish bait, and are also commonly thought to be the same as Tiger Salamander larvae.

Due to the similarities in their physical features, many prized Tiger Salamander larvae find themselves being sold off as fish bait under the guise of mudpuppies – on some cases, this deceit is even intentional. For a knowledgeable person, spotting the difference between a Tiger Salamander larvae and an aquatic Mudpuppy Is a simple matter of looking at the creature's toes. While Tiger Salamanders will boast of five toes on each of their hind feet, Mudpuppies develop only four.

Tiger Salamander larvae may also vary in size as young ones, with some growing to be larger and also more aggressive than other hatchlings. The larger larvae, also nicknamed Water Dogs, often find themselves being hooked in a net and sold off along with Mudpuppies as fishing bait or for pet trade.

3. Adult Male and Female Tiger Salamanders: Telling the Difference

To the unknowing eye, adult male and female Tiger Salamanders may be difficult to tell apart, mostly due to the similarities in their markings. There are no outwardly coloration patterns that distinguish the two sexes, nor are there any visible primary or secondary sex traits on physical display. To the trained or even observant eye, however, this caudate can be identified as male or female at a single measured glance.

While both, the male and females will grow to almost similar lengths, the differences in their sexes can be determined by looking at their overall build and their tails. A sexually male mature Tiger Salamander has an overall slimmer build when compared to his female counterpart. Although still stocky, the male's torso appears somewhat streamlined when compared to the female. In addition, the males develop flatter tails than the females.

Female Tiger Salamanders, on the other hand, develop well-rounded torsos at the time of attaining sexual maturity. They may seem to be a little chubbier when compared to the male specimen, but in fact, have developed their bodies to adapt the process of mating and breeding that Tiger Salamanders engage in.

Perhaps the most visible distinguishing factor among the two sexes, however, can be spotted at the rear ends of the Tiger Salamander. As with many amphibians, these herps possess a cloaca, an area located at the bottom of the torso right behind the hind legs, serving the purpose of the rectum. What tell the males apart from the females is the size of the cloaca, with a margin large enough to clearly separate the two. The male Tiger Salamanders have a more visibly "swollen" or protruding cloaca when compared to the small ones found on female bodies.

Regardless of the sex of the Tiger Salamander, or the way in which its organs develop and shape, both sexes have been studied to attain sexual maturity in under a year. Completing sexual development and preparing for the process of mating and breeding, however, takes around four to five years.

4. Tiger Salamanders and the Reproductive Cycle

Tiger Salamanders, by nature, tend to be creatures who prefer the solitary life. Most at ease when they are tucked away in underground burrows, they find further solitude by fetching food during the nightly hours. Despite these tendencies, Tiger Salamanders seem to understand the need for strong social behavioural patterns at the time of mating. It is during the breeding season in the rainy months that we get to witness interesting personality traits among these amphibians.

Using the cold winter months to gather and conserve energy, Tiger Salamanders are among the first to emerge from their cosy abodes once the spring season arrives. Due to their slow and somewhat sluggish movements, the amphibians use the spring months to move to a water-body enclosed area ideal for mating as well as egg depositing.
This early departure for the community breeding pond is perhaps what lends the "early breeder" label to the Tiger Salamander species. Interestingly, it is the males who arrive at the breeding ponds, with the females making their way in once the males have sized up the competition. As applies across the animal kingdom, it is the most dominant of the males who win the opportunity to fertilize the eggs of the sexually mature females.

Docile and withdrawing during the non-breeding months, the Tiger Salamander males become extremely aggressive towards each other during the mating season. With the arrival of the females begins the contest to win over a female willing to carry the spermatophore – or sperm sack- of the male salamander. While most males will compete amongst themselves for the attention of the females, some males Tiger Salamanders will prefer, for various reasons to use wily and cunning means to approach the females.

These males salamanders often imitate female behaviour patterns and traits as a means to, both, avoid the attention of other male Tiger Salamanders, as well as get close to the females without startling or upsetting them. Not very surprisingly, these attention-grabbing tactics are observed to be employed by those males who are considered weaker by either themselves or the others. This sly mating tactic may help some male Tiger Salamanders slip by the radar of other males, but may not always be deemed an attractive trait by other females. Very few males that use cunning as a mating rituals find themselves successful- it is the overtly aggressive that are given preference.

Once a male Tiger Salamander has successfully fended off the competition and attracted the attention of his desired female mate, he engages her in a coaxing ritual, prompting her to pick up his spermatophore. This capsule created by and containing the male Tiger Salamanders sperm, is often deposited at the bottom of the breeding ponds right before the female is lured into picking it up. The act of creating and then depositing sperm-filled capsules is a trait the the Tiger Salamander shares with his other salamander cousins and arthropods.

A willing female Tiger Salamander picks up the spermatophore and carries it within her body, where it dissolves, fertilizes with the eggs, and is prepared to be deposited once again as fertilized egg pouches. Once courted, the female will take about 24 to 48 hours to lay the egg pouches and cover them with such materials as twigs for safety. Keeping in tune with their shy nocturnal natures, females often prefer to lay their egg pouches in the quieter hours of the night.

The average female Tiger Salamander will deposit around two or three such egg pouches at choice locations, where they hatch into larvae and metamorphose over the next few weeks. Depending on the subspecies of Tiger Salamander, each egg mass will contain anywhere between 25 and 50 eggs. In many instances, female Tiger Salamanders have been to observed to lay between a 100 and 1,000 eggs in a breeding season.

Choice spots for the safe deposit of egg pouches are safe crevices tucked safely underwater, such as underwater plants, submerged and sunken logs, the water-covered undersides of large rocks and stones, and in many urban settlements, masses of debris comfortably nestled under water. The eggs take anywhere between 19 and 50 days to hatch into larvae, with 28 days being the average hatching period among all Tiger Salamander species.

One major factor that has been observed at being a catalyst in the egg hatching, is the temperature of the water the egg masses have been deposited in. Regions with warmer climates and subsequently warmer water bodies are found to be an early hatching ground for Tiger Salamander eggs. Colder, icier waters, on the other hand, encourage delayed hatching, which is probably why tropical and temperate climates are preferred by many Tiger Salamander species. The hatched larvae use the comforts of the underwater environment to fully develop into land-breathing adults. This metamorphosis may take around 2 or 2.5 months, during which time the larvae survive underwater through external gills, developed for early breathing. The months of July and August prove to be ideal for this period of development, and many Tiger Salamanders are ready to make the move to terrestrial planes by the times winter months roll in.

Curiously not all Tiger Salamanders may deem it necessary to transition from water to land the same year. Some prefer to remain as aquatic larvae for the rest of the seasonal cycles, emerging on to land only after the following breeding season. While it takes under a year for several Tiger Salamanders to develop into land-breathing adults, most of these amphibians reach the adult stage of sexual maturity only at the age of 4 or 5 years.

By the time the first winter months arrive, many newly-adult Tiger Salamanders will have moved a long distance away from their spot of hatching, in search of a cosy burrow-friendly area that will allow them to feed and hibernate. However, belonging to the family of

Ambystomatidae, they possess a sense of loyalty to their birthplaces, and will want to make the journey to that breeding pond for subsequent reproduction.

Some Tiger Salamanders, displaying their sexually competitive and aggressive traits, are also observed to use the later part of the winter months to begin courtship rituals with their female counterparts. This act makes it easy for the Salamander couple to begin the process of traveling to the breeding pond and depositing fertilized eggs once the spring season arrives. If the Tiger Salamander chooses, at its time of sexual maturity, to revisit its place of birth for breeding, it many often find that the journey to its breeding pond has now become challenging.

Owing to vast changes and development in the urban terrains of the North American continent, many Tiger Salamanders find that their journey back to the breeding ponds are now filled with such obstacles as construction debris, open traffic-filled roads and even residences. Despite these obstacles, many Tiger Salamanders will still make the arduous and eventful – if dangerous – trip back to their breeding grounds. Their devotion to the process of reproduction is further evidenced by their willingness to make the mating journey despite their otherwise shy and sluggish natures.

It is still not exactly known how Tiger Salamanders memorize, and then successfully relocate, their breeding grounds. Some studies, however, have theorized that these amphibians use a complex technique of polarizing the light of the sun to map out venues and routes. Adding to these challenges, Tiger Salamanders have further obstacles by their preferences to travel at nightly hours, preferring to hide safely underground during the active hours of the day.

It is perhaps because of the complications caused by the sum of the obstacles, that most Tiger Salamanders are observed to have only a 50 per cent chance of successfully breeding more than once in their lifetime.

5. The Curious Case of Tiger Salamander Larvae Survival

Once Tiger Salamander eggs hatch into larvae, the young ones take at least a little over two months to complete the metamorphosis from water-breathing gilled hatchlings to land-breathing adults. During this period, based on the spot chosen by the mother at the time of egg-laying, larvae will depend on the food and water resources readily available in their immediate surroundings as a means of survival and development.

In an ideal setting, such as a secluded forested area, the larvae should be supplied with plenty of food sources through running sources of water filled with tiny fish, ticks, fleas and other digestible edibles. In many cases, however, especially in the recent times of urban restructuring and development, female Tiger Salamanders may not always be able to guarantee consistent food for the larvae through their metamorphosis. During these times, the Salamander larvae rely on each other for growth and development – by becoming cannibalistic.

In accordance with the theory of survival displayed by nearly every species of animal, it is the stronger larvae that will prey on their weaker siblings, often when confronted with no other food source. Labeled "Cannibal Morphs", these larvae differ from the weaker Salamanders not only in character, but also in terms of resulting physical development.

Cannibal morphs have, in most cases, observed to grow to develop larger heads and bigger mouths when compared to their non-cannibal counterparts. In addition, these cannibal adults also display a set of fully-developed teeth, most probably sharpened by early cannibalistic practices. Probably owing to the highly enriched nourishment provided by their siblings, cannibal morphs also tend to develop at a faster rate and undergo metamorphosis at an earlier stage than the non-cannibal Tiger Salamanders. In addition, they also tend to retain the larger physical traits first displayed pre-metamorphosis.

While turning cannibal may seem like the only available option for Tiger Salamander survival in food-depleted areas, their transition from water to land is also obstacled by the seemingly new terrain they have to traverse. We have already seen how this event continues to be a lifelong challenge for many adult Tiger Salamanders. A solution that easily bypasses the need for this transition, while still developing into adults, is to simply remain aquatic through their lifetime!

Neotenes are those Tiger Salamanders that prefer the comforts of the aquatic life to the unknown challenges of the life on land. These Tiger Salamanders further cement their stay underwater by retaining their gills as a breathing device. They also skip undergoing the physical changes needed for survival on land, holding on to their larvae-state and focusing instead on attaining sexual maturity.

While turning neotenic may seem like an unlikely choice for Tiger Salamanders to make, it often proves to be advantageous to their physical traits, as well as to the longevity of their lives. Neotenic Tiger Salamanders have been studied to grow metamorphose to a larger size than their terrestrial counterparts, growing up to 15 inches, even longer on occasion. Furthermore, neotenic Tiger Salamanders, whether in the wild or in captivity, have been observed to live a long and healthy life of up to 25 years – almost an entire decade worth of difference when compared to the 10 to 15 years granted to their terrestrial cousins.

Whether they make the choice to turn cannibalistic, neotenic, or stick with the transition into non-salamander eating, land-breathing adults, all Tiger Salamanders will eventually make the common choice to breed solely in the rainy months near water bodies where they were first born – as many Ambystomatidae do.

Chapter Three: Understand your Tiger Salamander

1.   Tiger Salamanders and Natural Habitat

The Tiger Salamander may be a secretive and shy amphibian, but is certainly not scarce in its availability around the United States. This beautiful and adaptable creature can be spotted all over North America, from the eastern extremities of Mexico to the Rocky Mountains and even parts of Canada in the north. The only areas across the North American continent beyond the adaptable reaches of even the Tiger Salamander are the challenging terrains of the Appalachian mountains, the Great Basin, New England and the northern region of Canada.

The Tiger Salamander, in fact, shows such a preference for the comfortable terrain and climates of North American regions, that the state of South Dakota is known to be a favoured habitat of this amphibian – indeed, Tiger

Salamanders are arguably the only species of salamanders to naturally inhabit the state. You may happen across the majestic Gray Tiger Salamander in the south-eastern parts of South Dakota, or may even spot the more common Blotched Tiger Salamander while taking a stroll along the Missouri river.

Freely available Tiger Salamander larvae along marshy river banks and amidst large fields in large quantities make them a prized form of bait among the fishing community. This has led to different species Tiger Salamanders being shipped across the United States, far from their areas of origination. With passing time and successful breeding attempts, tracing the true area of origination for many Tiger Salamanders has become an almost ambiguous matter.

The current status of Tiger Salamanders as valued fishing bait has also attention of several environmental lobbies across regions in North America. In some states, these shy amphibians are labelled as "endangered" and find themselves protected by local laws.

2.   Living Conditions

The Tiger Salamander, being a member of the Mole Salamander family, possesses a particular fondness for burrows and the act of burrowing. The need for a comfortable underground shelter – whether to breed, feed, hide or simply hibernate, forms much of a Tiger Salamander's existence.

While physically equipped to dig out a comfortable burrow for itself from piles of soft earth, a Tiger Salamander is just as content inhabiting the burrows of other, smaller mammals, invertebrates and arthropods. An endorser of the "home invasion" technique, a Tiger Salamander that has just preyed on crayfish or small rodents may simply settle themselves amidst the dwellings of their meal.

The act of choosing a suitable burrow, for a Tiger Salamander, is more than just a display of their characteristic instincts. This species of amphibian seems especially aware to the ideal living conditions provided by underground burrows. Whether the Tiger Salamander will dig the burrow himself, or pick one out form the several abandoned ones, an ideal home will be located around 2 feet from the surface. This depth provides an optimum distance from the surface, with the right amount of moisture and coolness permeating the burrow.

Apart from finding the ideal burrow, another natural phenomenon that drives the Tiger Salamander's existence is the act of breeding. Coinciding with the rainy months between July and September, a Tiger Salamander will only emerge from hibernation to travel to a nearby water body and participate in the ritual of mating. It is for this reason, perhaps, that Tiger Salamanders are most easily spotted across North America during the months of July and August.

It is interesting to note that Tiger Salamanders, as adults, are largely terrestrial creatures. They do, however, prefer the relative safety offered by shallow water banks when it is time to lay their eggs. New born Tiger Salamanders spend much of their early developmental stages in water, making them aquatic. It is only around the time of maturation do they make the transition from water to land. This adaptability opens the Tiger Salamander up to a variety of living conditions.

During the breeding season, Tiger Salamanders tend to gather around such water bodies as ponds, marshes and flowing streams of water. These water bodies would ideally be located in secluded forested areas, but Tiger Salamander eggs have also been found along urban embankments and roadside ditches. Despite being mostly land-friendly as adults, Tiger Salamanders have also proven to be adept swimmers, further making the banks of water bodies hospitable to their feeding and reproducing needs.

Once the mating and breeding season is done, the Tiger Salamander makes its way to land with soft earth that can be dug and burrowed, if it hasn't already been done by other creatures. These burrows are commonly located in large fields, prairies or forested areas protected by layers of leafy cover on the forest floor. Ideal burrows are those that complement the secretive and shy nature of the Tiger Salamanders.

3.   Tiger Salamanders and the Ecology

It may seem easy to undermine, and often ignore the importance of a species such as the Tiger Salamander in the thriving of an ecosystem – and most often, we do. This, however, does not deter the members of this species from playing an important role in maintaining the vital balance needed in their natural surroundings.

As is evidenced by their feeding, sheltering and breeding preferences, Tiger Salamanders tend to inhabit areas with tropical and temperate climates. In a wild setting, these climates also provide to be extremely hospitable to a diverse array of flora and fauna. Plant Life, especially that of medicinal, nutritional and cosmetic value, is seen to be bountiful in such an environment. Pests such as ticks, bugs and other tiny insects that prey on plant life form the perfect feed for many Tiger Salamanders.

Bigger Tiger Salamanders also feed on small rodents that consume the plants in their surroundings. By playing the role of the larger predator, Tiger Salamanders help keep useful plant life safe from the mouths of others feeders. This simple act also increases the spread of greenery in the area, helping plants to pump out more oxygen.

To those people who own even the tiniest pieces of cultivable land, Tiger Salamanders prove to be farmer-friendly and an effective yet cheap form of natural pest control. By turning common everyday predators into food sources, Tiger Salamanders prove themselves worthy of keeping around.

Unbeknownst to them, Tiger Salamanders further help in the supply of essential oxygen by preying on those species known to emit carbon gases. Such small animals as beetles, earthworms, ants and even the lethargic snails are all known to be tiny contributors towards the larger problem of carbon emission into the atmosphere. With the help of Tiger Salamanders, however, the spread of the carbon gases are kept in check even before they are emitted into the atmosphere.

Despite these uses to their immediate ecosystem, Tiger Salamanders often find themselves fighting to survive among larger species and mostly, among humans. Their preferred natural habitats in temperate and tropical climates are also favoured by humans and other larger species. With urbanization taking away most of their underground burrows, even replacing soft earth for concrete, Tiger Salamanders often find themselves without safe shelters and breeding ponds.

As creatures who prefer the quiet of the nocturnal hours, many Tiger Salamanders across states in North America find themselves exposed to large predators such as snakes or big birds, if they successfully hatching and metamorphose into adults. It is no wonder, then, that these severely depleting salamanders have had to receive additional protection from several state laws to ensure their continued survival.

Chapter Four: The Tiger Salamander as a Pet

1.   Pet Tiger Salamanders and Legal considerations

For those who like the unique perspective on domestication that Tiger Salamanders offer, the caudates make for easy-to-please, laidback companions. If you are one of these people, you may also take a special interest in the process through which your Tiger Salamander reaches you. Vast though their natural range may be, not all Tiger Salamanders are up for picking and housing at the individual's will.

The dwindling number of several subspecies of the Tiger Salamander means that they receive special protection from many states across the North American continent. While some of these rules lay certain restrictions on the hunting and possession of these caudates, other laws may prohibit the acquisition or ownership of any Salamanders altogether. Therefore, in order to protect yourself, is it essential that you understand which members of the Tiger Salamander family are available to legally hunt, buy or possess.

It wouldn't be surprising if you had your heart set on owning a California Tiger Salamander or a Sonoran Tiger Salamander. You must know, however, that hunting or possessing one of these majestic caudates is illegal in most parts of the United States. Furthermore, the Eastern Tiger Salamander is especially protected by the states of New Jersey and California, with ownership or possession of this caudate deemed illegal.

You may want to divert your attention to other varieties, such as the blotted, barred or blotches versions of the Tiger Salamander. Be warned, however, that even these options may not be a possibility in California, a state that prohibits the possession of any species of mole salamander.

If you do live in a state that permits you to house a Tiger Salamander, you may find yourself turning to the legal pages once again, should you make certain decisions regarding your pet's development. Certain phenomena, such as metamorphosis, can be chemically induced by laboratories, in case the Tiger Salamander has not made the transition and the owner wishes otherwise. While perfectly safe, the legality of this procedure still differs from state to state, and it is best to ensure you are in the legal safe zone before you make such decisions.

To make matters more complicated, should you choose to simply go looking for the larvae deposited along the watery catchments in your area, ensure that you are legally permitted to do so. Many states require their residents to own active fishing licenses before acquiring larvae and eggs of any kind for themselves. States that do allow you to collect egg masses and then raise them will also probably need you to show a registered fishing license first. You should definitely consider the legal consequences of hunting for a group of Tiger Salamander larvae, and have the right kind of education on the subject.

The question then arises, "can I legally own a Tiger Salamander at all in the United States?" If you're willing to be a little flexible in your choices, in many areas, you most certainly can. A quick perusal of the local Game and Wildlife laws that govern each county or state reveals that these governments mostly work to protect those species of Tiger Salamander that are native to their land. It is generally only these species that will have specific guidelines that dictate the terms of their sale, acquisition or ownership.

Therefore, while you still may not be able to either bring home or keep an Eastern Tiger Salamander in the state of Ohio, you most certainly can give a safe and happy home to one of the many healthy barred or blotched Tiger Salamander varieties. Consider this option in other areas in the United States, and you may find that owning a Tiger Salamander is not as tricky a process as you thought.

If you aren't sure whom to ask for the right legal information concerning the acquisition and ownership of Tiger Salamanders as pets, you can find plenty of literature on this subject on the Internet. Each state's government website will list out all particulars surrounding the purchase and possession of flora and fauna. Browse through the Game and Wildlife department pages for the most accurate and up-to-date information.

2.   Larvae or Adult – The right age to bring home a Tiger Salamander

Once you have assured yourself – through adequate research and homework – of the legality of bringing home a Tiger Salamander, you can start to think about the specifics of your pet. Before you sit down to chalk out your next few years with your caudate, it's wise to consider the age of the amphibian that best suits your preferences, and lifestyle.

The first thing to remember about Tiger Salamanders is that they live out their existence on two surfaces – first water, and then land. As the caregiver of a creature whose life cycles determine such basic activities as breathing, you have to be ready to usher your pet through each developmental stage.

If you happen to acquire, or wish to purchase Tiger Salamander larvae, therefore, it is best that you make arrangements for an aquatic environment, essential for younger caudates' survival. Proper food, environmental settings and privacy should help your young one grow into a beautiful sexually mature adult within a couple of years. Bear in mind, however, that your Tiger Salamander larvae may not always metamorphose into a terrestrial animal.

As the owner of a young Tiger Salamander, you prepare yourself not only for the transition from an aquatic to terrestrial environment, but also for the possibility that your pet may skip metamorphosis altogether. Neotenes have their own set of developmental advantages, with the tendency to grow bigger and live longer than their terrestrial siblings. They may, however, never develop patterns and colourings as striking as the land-breathing adults.

If you had your heart set on raising a fully-metamorphosed amphibian, you will find that there is virtually no way to enforce this transition in the Tiger Salamander. While some laboratories and services have been able to trigger metamorphosis by administering iodine to developing Tiger Salamanders, ensure that you understand the safety and legality of this procedure in your area before you proceed.

Otherwise, you can guarantee bringing home a terrestrial Tiger Salamander by picking one up once it is in the last stages of, or has completed metamorphosis. While you may miss out on the young developmental stages of the caudate growth, you can still enjoy a lasting and enriching bond with the non-interfering adult.

Furthermore, if you have the time, space and commitment, you can ensure that you raise at least one land-breathing adult by bringing home a small group of larvae. With the right care and space, you can prevent the larvae from turning cannibalistic and raise more than one healthy amphibian. If you then feel that you cannot care for more than one adult, many reputed vendors will be happy to buy adult Tiger Salamanders raised in captivity from you.

Many Tiger Salamander owners feel an almost parental responsibility towards their pets (as owners of all pets do), and prefer to let nature take its course in determining the amphibian's breathing patterns. If you, too, do not mind whether your caudate metamorphose into a land amphibian it remains aquatic, then the age of the Tiger Salamander should not be too much of a problem for you.

3. How many Tiger Salamanders should you house?

If you prefer the company of those animals that are content with being solitary, then the Tiger Salamander is an ideal pet for you. By nature, these shy caudates only feel the need for companionship during the mating and breeding season. They are not plagued by bouts of loneliness and for the better part of the year are perfectly happy with quiet surroundings and little opportunity for social interaction.

Provided you have the right housing and feeding conditions in place, you and your Tiger Salamander should share an easy companionship that lasts over a decade. Do not, however, be disappointed if you harboured the hope of housing more than one of the ambystoma. Shy though they may be, Tiger Salamanders, in many cases, willingly share their living quarters with others of their type. There are two primary requisites you will have to bear in mind to ensure the comfort and happiness of all the Salamanders:

sufficient food for each, along space enough to garner a feeling of personal privacy.

When in captivity, a Tiger Salamander requires a tank measuring around 40x20 cm (with a capacity of around 10 gallons) for it to comfortably burrow, forage and wander. With these approximate measurements in mind, you can select a tank with a capacity of around 20 gallons (75x40) cms to house an adult pair of Tiger Salamanders. This vivarium should give the caudates enough room to inhabit in seclusion or otherwise.

The size of your tank, along with your discipline as a food provider, will especially matter if your adults are cannibal morphs, or are in the growth and development stage. With cramped quarters and inconsistent feeding habits, the Tiger Salamander may become territorial and hungry, looking to each other as a food source. Conversely, adequate space to burrow, with shallow waters that prevent drowning, complemented by regular supply of fresh bait, will encourage healthy cohabitation between multiple Tiger Salamanders, should this be your choice.

On the whole, bringing home more than one Tiger Salamander is not a very large inconvenience – indeed, with the right environment, you may have little to do as a owner besides provide food and maintain a sterile environment. The biggest impact of purchasing over one of these caudates will be felt on your budget. A number of Tiger Salamanders will mean larger quantities of food, supplied constantly, most of which may not be easy to source, especially in urban areas. Furthermore, maintaining a clean and sterile environment for a group of amphibians with sensitive-to-handle skin is a challenging task.

Many owners who buy a group of Tiger Salamanders tend to make this decision before the caudates have metamorphosed, to avoid getting neotenes in the bargain. If, like them, you are particular about the nature of your Tiger Salamander, and prefer a land-breathing adult to a water-breathing one, you can either purchase a group of larvae, or buy a fully-developed adult.

Ultimately this shy caudate has been observed to prefer being a personal companion to being part of a bigger group, whether in the wild or in captivity. Its unique refusal to breed in captivity in most cases lessens your worry of finding the amphibian a mate. With the above factors in mind, it helps to take some time to consider how many of these beautiful amphibians you want to share your living space with.

4.   Tiger   Salamanders   and   commonly   asked questions

Will my Tiger Salamander shed its skin?

Yes it will, and it helps to know a little about this periodical phenomenon. As is common with many amphibians, Tiger Salamanders will shed their skin at regular intervals. This act is especially noticeable during the growth and development stages.

Every three to four weeks, the outermost layer of the Salamander's epidermis begins to peel away, making way for new skin. The shedding looks almost plastic-like in its appearance: it is thin, flimsy to touch, and is mostly translucent, almost transparent at sight.

This old skin usually peels away in one whole sheet, making its exit through the back end of the body. You will notice your Tiger Salamander using its hind legs to help propel the skin off its back. Don't be surprised, however, if you find the Tiger Salamander encouraging the skin towards its mouth, instead of shedding it away.

Keeping the behavior patterns of many caudates intact, Tiger Salamanders will often eat their shedding. Their skin is an easily available source of nutrients as well as moisture, while also being nature's mechanism of conserving this abundance of nutrition. In fact, feeding on their shedding could be considered almost essential to their survival.

The Tiger Salamander may not always consume all of its shedding, and the remains may harden and end up coating the surfaces around the vivarium. It is wise to clean away these sheddings, to prevent unnecessary chances of contamination to the environment.

Will my Tiger Salamander be a noisy pet?

For the most part, no. Tiger Salamanders will be almost noiseless pets to have. This convenience, if you are the type that relishes quiet, is aided by the lack of vocal chords, and even ears, in the Tiger Salamander's anatomy.

Therefore, with no vocalization skills to speak of, Tiger Salamanders should spend their days in relative silence. On rare occasions, however, you may hear a tiny sharp "squeal" emitted by your pet. This is mostly occur when the Salamander is picked up or feels tangibly disturbed by an external presence. While not common, it is believed that this sound is made by exerting air out through the Tiger Salamander's nares.

Will I need to place a drinking source for my Tiger Salamander?

Surprisingly, No. As a unique adaptive trait, Tiger Salamanders do not quench their thirst by drinking water through their mouths. Instead, they rely on their environment and surroundings to provide them with the moisture and hydration levels needed for their sustenance.

Tiger Salamanders absorb the moisture content from such sources as their shedding, the water from the bodies of their prey, as well as from the air around them seeping rough their skin. It is for the last reason, especially, that the need for a moist and slightly humid substrate becomes essential for your Tiger Salamander. Along with mimicking the caudate natural range, the moisture is literally a life-giver to your pet.

Will my Tiger Salamander bite me?

If it does, know that this "nip" was an accident. Tiger Salamanders are shy and docile by nature, never intentionally aggressive or volatile. The only events during which they will display overt signs of aggression are during the breeding seasons. Even then, this hostility is only targeted towards other males for brief periods.

If you do feel a "nip" from your Tiger Salamander, notice that is most probably occurs at mealtimes, just as you deposit the feed into the tank. Tiger Salamanders, especially once they recognize their feeders, will become excited when you arrive with live feed. If you house more than one Tiger Salamander in the same tank, they will try to compete with each other for the food. Sometimes this excitement may lead to them nipping at you in the hurry to grab the feed first.

In other cases, the Tiger Salamander may accidentally nip you while picking the feed, or may also mistake you fingers for worms (especially if they are wriggling rapidly). Do not interpret this for hostility from your pet. Furthermore, the nip itself is often virtually painless, and does not harm you.

If you do get nipped, you may feel a slight scraping sensation – this is caused by the teeth-like biters arranged in rows in the Tiger Salamander's mouth lining the upper and lower roofs, these jagged-edged appendages help the Tiger Salamanders grip their prey firmly by the neck, before snapping the neck and feeding on the bait.

Chapter Five: Selecting a Pet Tiger Salamander

Once you have done the required research, considered other options and finally settled on bringing home a Tiger Salamander, the next obvious step is to acquire a healthy specimen. While it may be relatively easy to pick up a another species of pet, such as a dog, duck or even a rabbit, Tiger Salamanders are slightly trickier to track down. Coupled with the varying laws that govern the purchase and possession of these caudates, it becomes important to give your pet a home without breaking rules or causing yourself disappointment.

Tiger Salamanders roam the expanse of the North American continent in large numbers, especially during the rainy months. If you currently reside, or have lived in a salamander-friendly zone, a line of these colorful amphibians darting across your backyard may have been a common sight. And despite their seeming abundance, Tiger Salamanders are actually an endangered species that require governmental intervention to survive. So you may not be able to simply "adopt" a stray Tiger Salamander that strays into your room if your state does not permit it.

If catching Tiger Salamanders from the wild is a legally sketchy way to acquire them, the next suggestion would be to simply breed Tiger Salamanders for sale as pets. This effort, though carried out extensively, exhaustively and over a period of years, has not been very successful. For reasons still being determined, Tiger Salamanders are notorious for their near inability to breed in captivity.

Attempts to encourage and enable mating have been met with failure in an overwhelming number of instances. You will find an array of literature documenting Tiger Salamander breeding trials, that included breeding neotenes in captivity and providing the caudates with ideal breeding conditions in captivity year-long. Efforts went as far as to administer hormonal treatments to the amphibians, with no sustained successful result.

This set of circumstances brings you, as a potential owner, back to relying on those areas that do allow purchase and acquisition of Tiger Salamanders from the wild. If you are lucky, your state may also grant you the fishing permits necessary to visit a breeding pond and collect your larvae. As a member of the elite club that can bring this docile ambystoma home, you then have a few options at your disposal.

1.   Acquiring Tiger Salamander Larvae through the Local Fishing Trade

As many Tiger Salamander owners have discovered, one of the most popular sources for acquiring your own smiling caudate is through the fishing community in your area. In those states with a heavy fishing culture owing to the abundance of water bodies with rich ecosystems, Tiger Salamander larvae are a cheap and prized source of bait. Small, nutritious and available in large quantities, these larvae are shipped across state borders – such is their economic value.

The handing over of Tiger Salamander larvae as bait may not always be intentional, however. Easily available though they may be, they are often mistaken for similar-looking aquatic creatures called Mudpuppies. It is the Mudpuppies that are the intended bait, with Tiger Salamander larvae being picked up as the former due to their appearance. Since the larvae and collected and sold at wholesale rates to traders, you can easily amass a handful of larvae at reasonable prices, with chances of many being Tiger Salamanders.

And if you know the trick that helps differentiate a Tiger Salamander from a Mudpuppy – the extra toe on the hind feet – then you can further avoid picking Mudpuppies by spotting your companion from the lot. When you do get lucky through the bait trade, and can find yourself larvae at fishing bait shops, these will most likely be of the blotched or barred variety.

It may seem like the fishing trade method is not the most reliable way of acquiring a Tiger Salamander, and that's probably because it is. The fishing community can guarantee you a handful of larvae to choose from, but may not be able to accurately help you with the species that you have picked up, or even guarantee that the Tiger Salamander will metamorphose, should you want it. This source is only popular due to its convenience. If you want to exercise a little more control over your purchase, the next best source for your Tiger Salamander would be a vendor.

2.   Picking up a Tiger Salamander from a Vendor

As is with the purchase of most pets, your safest bet when it comes to acquiring your Tiger Salamander is a reputed vendor in your area. It is from this source that you have your best chance at picking a healthy specimen in the species of your choice.

Most vendors will have acquired their Tiger Salamander as larvae either from other states, or from within their own territory. If your vendor does have Tiger Salamanders for you to choose from, or can arrange the same, they will ensure they this caudate have been handed to you bearing all legal and medical requirements in mind. This does not necessarily mean that every vendor will ethically sell you a Tiger Salamander, however.

It is best that you have your background information on the ambystoma ready before you make a trip to the local vendor. Knowledge on the general physical traits, appearance, and the legal permits concerning the ownership and sale of the amphibian can help you avoid possibility of a scam. Some vendors, whether out of ignorance or poor choice of business ethics, will sell you Mudpuppies under the guise of Tiger Salamanders. To the unknowing buyer, this Mudpuppy, or Waterdog, could be a neotene or larvae.

Doing your background research also allows you to determine which breed of Tiger Salamander most appeals to you. Reputed and trusted vendors will have Tiger Salamanders on sale mostly towards the end of the breeding season onwards, from the late parts of summer to the early months of fall. This coincides with the metamorphosis stage of the Tiger Salamander larvae, which helps reveals the species of the caudate, and also reveals whether it will make the transition to a land breathing adult or remain neotenic.

It is, in fact, very wise to make your purchase during this stage, and to select a metamorph for yourself, instead of a fully-grown adult. You will get to clearly tell the subspecies of the Tiger Salamander, as well as take on the responsibility to help it develop and grow to its full potential.

3.   "Herping" a Tiger Salamander from the Wild

We have already discussed how stringent state laws can make the hunting, purchase, or ownership of a Tiger Salamander a tricky affair, particularly within the United States. If you do happen to live in a state that allows the possession of a Tiger Salamander as a pet, and have hit the additional jackpot of acquiring the fishing license necessary for collecting larvae, then you may want to give hunting for this caudate, or "herping", a try.

Before you make your plans to "help" your first Tiger Salamander, take some time to acquaint yourself with the general habits of the species you wish to bring home. A little prior information on the movement and behavior patterns of the Tiger Salamanders in your area can turn your herping adventure into a simple, rewarding task. Some questions you should be able to answer comfortably include:

• What types/breeds of Tiger Salamanders are available for herping?

• Is it, firstly legal, and secondly convenient, to herp Tiger Salamander larvae or adults?

• Where, in your area, does the Tiger Salamander burrow and rest?

• Where does the Tiger Salamander forage for food sources?

• Which months do the Tiger Salamanders emerge for breeding and foraging?

• Where is the nearest breeding pond?

• What time of the day do the Tiger Salamanders emerge for travel or foraging?

Armed with this information, you are now ready to go looking for a Tiger Salamander pet in your surroundings. The success rate of herping a Tiger Salamander varies from person to person; some have managed to acquire a caudate within days of planning to house it, while others have had tougher luck spotting and capturing these shy creatures. Here are some tips that should help make your herping experience easier and convenient for you:

Before you set out to capture your Tiger Salamander to bring home, understand that you may not always spot an adult out in the open. Preferring to forage and wander during the late hours of the night, you will have more luck chancing upon larvae than metamorphosed adults.

Be prepared to look for these caudates in a diverse array of environments; Tiger Salamanders will comfortably inhabit lush, dense forests with as much ease as dry and arid deserts.

It is best not to spend your winter months looking for Tiger Salamanders. Since these amphibians emerge from their hibernative state mostly to breed, you will find plenty of adults and young out in the open during the rainy months .

When the Tiger Salamanders do emerge to travel to the breeding ponds, or even forage for food, they prefer to do it in the late hours of night and the early hours of morning. These are your best opportunities to catch one unaware

If a horde of Tiger Salamanders with easy pickings is what you prefer, try and pan your herping trip in the months of March and April. It is during this time that they make their way, usually in large numbers, to a common breeding pond, and move slowly enough for you to pick one up for yourself

If you live in an urban area in a state that is native to a species of Tiger Salamander, you may have already spotted a line of these caudates traveling determinedly across a busy street, your backyard and along sewers. State laws permitting, open urban areas that serve as migration routes give you the perfect opportunity to pick your Tiger Salamander.

If you do live in urban settlements, keep a look out for "migrators" across your lawns, ask neighbours to inform you if they spot one, and search for larvae and adults in water-logged areas such as ditches and potholes on abandoned roads.

Even within a state, the range of Tiger Salamanders may not always extend across all areas. Some parts may have a dense caudate population, with others witnessing no amphibian sightings. Consult your local government records to properly understand the natural range of Tiger Salamanders in your territory, and prevent a wasted expedition.

The Great Plains region of the United States – Colorado, Kansas, Nebraska, Montana, New Mexico, North Dakota, South Dakota, Oklahoma, Texas and Wyoming – along with the Alberta, Manitoba and Saskatchewan provinces of Canada, usually witness their first Tiger Salamander sightings immediately after the first heavy thunder showers that signal the end of the winter months. If you live in these areas, use the early rains as a signal to begin planning your herping activity.

If it is an Eastern Tiger Salamander that you're looking for, you should have the best luck in the later winter and early spring months. The larvae of these caudates are, in fact, found all year round in large collections of 50-200 per pouch.

Whether larvae or adults, all Tiger Salamanders can be safely caught using an adequately-sized fishing net, and then deposited into the prepared tank at the earliest.

4.   Selecting a Healthy Tiger Salamander specimen

Whether you pick out your smiling herp from the wild or select him from a reputed reptile and amphibian dealer, it is likely that your Tiger Salamander has not been in captivity before. Its time as a member of the natural ecosystem, and then having to exist in close quarters with other animals may have some effects on its appearance, its behaviour, and mostly its health.

You do not want to bring home a specimen that is ailing, temperamental and possibly cannibalistic. Not only will the amphibian be stressed and have difficulties adjusting to your environment, may unknown infections and diseases spread from the pet to you and your housemates. A healthy Tiger Salamander is a joy to raise and pet, and you should not have to fret over the physical condition of your caudate after your strenuous efforts to bring it home. To avoid such inconveniences, it is best that you give a small general examination to the Tiger Salamander you intend to herp or purchase. Here are some tips to help you select a healthy pet for yourself:

1.   Carry a pair of disposable latex gloves with you, for safe handling and picking of the Tiger Salamander. Bare hands, especially if they've   been   exposed   to germs, may be too distressing for the sensitive skin of the Tiger Salamander, may also transmit micro bodies from the amphibian's dermis to yours.

2.   The first sign of a prime Caudate candidate is a clear and healthy skin. A healthy Salamander coat has markings and patterns that are bold, striking and well-developed. Any discolorations on the skin could signal an underlying infection.

3.   Check the skin for visible blisters or sores. As with discolorations,   these could also be indicators of infections, possibly caused by bacteria or fungi. Such infections should be spotted as early as possible, as they escalate from passive bodies to attacking invaders very abruptly, often leaving the Tiger Salamander incapable of receiving treatment or cure.

4.   Gently examine the entire length of the caudate body, along with the limbs and digits, to check for wounds,

scratches or bite marks from other animals. As creatures of the open, freshly-caught Tiger Salamanders may have a small nip or two. If superficial, these can be easily treated.

5.   Your Tiger Salamander may also exhibit wound or bite marks if kept in captivity with many others of the same species in areas such as pet stores. Extended periods of living in cramped quarters like buckets and community tanks may upset the caudates and cause a few territorial tussles. Again, superficial and newer wounds can be cleaned and treated. Wounds that have set in and are left untreated may become infected and, in turn, adversely affect the caudate health.

6.   When placed on its feet, your potential pet should display relative signs of activity. It may try and scoot to the nearest hiding spot or burrow, or may display eager food foraging and feeding habits. An active Tiger Salamander is a healthy Salamander, and one that will give you a fulfilling companionship.

5.   Consideration Checklist before bringing home a Tiger Salamander

Docile and non-interfering though they may be, it may seem like a lot of consideration is required before acquiring a Tiger Salamander, and rightly so. Tiger Salamanders may be endangered in many parts, but they are also solitary creatures, built for survival. The choice to bring one out of the wild and into captivity, therefore, places the responsibility of their care on you.

If you can provide the same amount of attention and care that you would to a conventional pet, such as a dog, cat or

even a school of fish, then caring for a Tiger Salamander will be an easy ask. If you are expecting the same level of interaction with your Salamander that a dog or cat would provide, then an amphibian may not be your choice of pet.
If your desire to bring home a Tiger Salamander sustains all the considerations placed, both social and legal, then you may find a long-term friend in this caudate. Here is a checklist of questions that should help you better make your choice.

* Do state laws permit the herping and/or possession of a pet Tiger Salamander?
* If yes, are the permitted Tiger Salamander species on your list of preferences?
* Is your environment hospitable to house a Tiger Salamander?
* Can you set up the required vivarium and ensure its sterile environment?
* Can you provide flexible caring techniques for the Tiger Salamander during metamorphosis?
* Can you provide food easily and consistently for the pet?
* Are you comfortable interacting with/handling live animals (earthworms, crickets) to feed your pet?
* Are you comfortable directly feeding the live bait to your pet?
* Can you entrust the care of your pet Tiger Salamander to someone while you're unavailable (for short and long-term periods)?
* Are your living companions, should you have any (family members, roommates, landlord) comfortable with a Tiger Salamander in the premises?

Ultimately, bringing home a Tiger Salamander should be a decision that enhances the lives of both, the amphibian, and you.

Chapter Six: Housing your Tiger Salamander

The size, design and contents of your vivarium create a significant impact on the Tiger Salamander that you intend to house in it. Easily adaptable though they might be, the docile Tiger Salamander may need to find itself in familiar surroundings to overcome its initial feelings of displacement and disorientation. How you maintain the constructed habitat of your caudate will then largely determine the health and well-being of your pet.

The consideration and thought you put towards deciding how many Tiger Salamanders you want to house, and at what age you choose to bring them home, are key factors that come into play when setting up a housing environment for the caudates. While adult Tiger Salamanders will need a large tank to burrow and wander around comfortably in, younger aquatic larvae will require a higher water content to ensure their survival.

Furthermore, all Tiger Salamanders will require accessories that can double up as hiding spots or places of retreat. The following are factors for you to keep in mind as you begin compiling the contents of your Tiger Salamander vivarium:

- Space is a key component of your vivarium; adult Tiger Salamanders grow up to around 13 inches in length, and require plenty of personal space to enable their solitary burrowing habits. Even if you house a solitary Tiger Salamander, an adult will require a considerably bigger tank than ones reserved for other amphibians – around 10 gallons is a good average size.

- If you plan on housing two adult Salamanders together, particularly male, ensure that your enclosure has a volume of at least 15 to 20 gallons.

- Adult terrestrial Tiger Salamanders thrive in a woodland setting, so designing your vivarium around this theme is ideal for most Tiger Salamanders. A coco husk substrate has been recommended by many owners as a complement to the woodland environment.

- Tiger Salamander larvae, on the other hand, will require an aquatic setup in the vivarium – in other words, an aquarium.

- The aquarium housing the caudates during their larval phase will have to be filled up to 15 cms (6 inches) water, and be heated to a temperature of approximately 19 degrees Celsius (67 degrees Fahrenheit).

- The aquarium will also require such components as a powerful filter and soft-edged rocks scattered around the floor, for optimum thriving of your larval pets

- A choice of hiding spots, both for Tiger Salamander larvae and adults, are of utmost importance. You will need to incorporate such elements as makeshift logs, plant pots and piles of stones for burrowing and tunneling. Such elements also add to the aesthetic appeal of the vivarium

- Such components as moss, peat sphagnum moss and certain varieties of live plants should also be part of an ideal coco husk substrate, and will need to be designed to the caudate preference.

- You will have to gain knowledge of those elements that may may harmful to the vivarium and the general well-being of your Tiger Salamander. Not all live plants may contribute towards a healthy environment, and components such as gravel on the floor may cause harm to the caudates.

- Every element that is added to the vivarium and the Tiger Salamander's habitat will need to be cleaned and disinfected as a precaution against illness. Chlorine-water solution rinses, followed by an additional round of rinsing in fresh water will have to be undertaken on a regular basis.

- Docile though they may be, Tiger Salamanders are also curious by nature and enjoy exploring their surroundings. They have shown listlessness in captivity when exposed to the same setting over time. To ensure that your pet is engaged and alert, you will need to regularly make a few shifts and changes to the environment.

1.   Setting up the Vivarium

When setting up your vivarium, you will have to firstly consider the size of the tank intended to house your caudates. This is determined by the number of Tiger Salamanders you will house together. Ideally, you should intend to keep one adult Tiger Salamander per enclosure, two at the very most.

You will find that a tank with a volume of approximately 15 gallons, or measuring 24 inches in length and 12 inches in height (61x30x30cm) houses one adult Tiger Salamander comfortably. If a pair of adults is your intention, add another 5 gallons to the tank to create adequate space for privacy and interaction.

Your Tiger Salamander will need to believe that the tank is the entirety of its ecosystem; finding out that there is a chaotic world right outside its premises could cause stress. For this reason, three sides of the tank should preferably be taped with calming and stress-reducing posters, such as a peaceful aquatic background, terrestrial scenery, or even an opaque black or dark blue sheet of chart paper. In addition, the top of the vivarium will require a screen covering with hinges that allow ventilation and access to the tank, but prevent the Tiger salamanders from wandering outside the vivarium and escaping.

Your next priority should be directed towards the flooring of the vivarium. Remember that your Tiger Salamander is part of the Ambystoma family; this encourages his love for burrowing and tunnelling underground cocoons that gives them privacy. The bed of your vivarium will need to similarly mimic a soft flooring that encourages burrowing. This will help prevent the Tiger Salamander from becoming stressed, and will also encourage it to stay physically active and curious.

The ideal substrate prescribed for an adult Tiger Salamander tank is a coco husk substrate, a mixture of coconut and husk fibres embedded into soft soil. Mixtures such as coconut husk and mulch from trees such as cypress had also found to be ideal. Among other popular choices with the Tiger Salamander owners community are such safe and biodegradable options such as top soil, leaf litter and eco-friendly ready-to-use soil mixtures sold by many pet stores.

What must be avoided in a Tiger salamander's habitat, are small gravelly pieces of debris that can be ingested easily. Tiger Salamanders enjoy nothing more than poking at the objects in its environment, eating whatever takes its fancy. Pieces of gravel, sharp jagged stones, etc. may become lodged in the caudate throat or cause rupture in the digestive tract before embedding itself there.

It is also essential that the substrate be able to withhold large amounts of moisture for an extended period of time without becoming too damp and infestation-friendly. This make a coco husk substrate additionally appealing. You can also place your vivarium at a slightly tilted angled, with the tank itself supported on a base at the tilt. By doing so, you allow the excess water to drain towards the bottom of the tank instead of seeping through the bedding, leaving the substrate dry for a longer period of time.

Finally, your substrate will need as many nooks, crannies and hiding spots as you can cram in without completing obstructing the caudate movement. Tiger Salamander love to hide and wander about areas with flat, broad bases; these spaces seem to bring them comfort. They also add an ornamental and aesthetic appeal to your vivarium, making it a pleasing zone for your pet, as well as for you.

Consider such accessories as small logs, driftwood, flat large stones, small rocks, piece of cork, etc. Remember that all items will need to be cleaned, washed and sterilized before depositing into the vivarium. You can also set up either artificial or even live plants. Consider, however, that artificial plants will only add decorative value, while live plants will help further the habitat. Not all live plants may be suitable for the terrarium, however, and will all have to be planted firmly into the bed so as not to be disturbed by the burrowing caudates.

2.   The Importance of the Right Substrate

Of all the factors that will make up a vibrant and thriving vivarium for your Tiger salamander, the substrate is perhaps the most important of them all. Though a simple setting for the flooring of your tank, the substrate affects nearly every aspect of life in the enclosure – from the humidity, to the temperature, to even the spread or control of diseases and infection in the tank.

An ideal substrate is one that adheres to the nocturnal ambystoma nature of the Tiger Salamander. With features and a set-up that encourages burrowing, foraging and estivation, it is the right kind of substrate that will make the difference between a content and stressful life for your pet caudate. The following are some features of the ideal substrate, along with the impacts they have on the overall environment:

1. The primary purpose of the substrate is to contain generous amounts of moisture and water, without having to be changed regularly. The need for an absorbent substrate is also essential for the absorption of hydration through the Tiger Salamander's pores.

2. The substrate, while being moisture-absorbent, should not become so moist that it lumps together to form balls of earth. It should also not be so dry that the bed floor becomes cracked with dehydration.

3. An ideal substrate with the right amount of moisture often has the smell of fresh moist earth after new rains. This smell is also a good indicator of the long-term health of your substrate.

4. In addition, the substrate should be plough able enough that the Tiger salamander can use it for burrowing and tunnelling.

5. An ideal substrate should be able to both, contain, and then   disintegrate any food or fecal remains, along with skin shedding
    .

6. The right kind of substrate is gentle enough not to be abrasive or allergic to skin contact, whether human or amphibian. Such surfaces as jagged wood, sharp stones or rusty cage edges may lessen the appeal of the enclosure and make it more hostile for the caudate.

7. In order to allow moisture to collect at the bottom for the Tiger salamander to absorb, without dampening the tank, the substrate should be light yet firm enough that the vivarium can be placed at a slightly tilted angle.

8. The substrate should cover about 4 inches of the tank from the bottom surface upwards. This surface should also not be packed in too tightly with soil. Rather, it must be carefully layered and loosely   packed   to allow Tiger salamander to burrow through the floor with ease.

9. The best types of substrate that fulfil the above requirement are found to be coco-fibre substrates, mostly sold in tightly-packed bricks in pet stores or online trade portals. It can be unpacked and then touched up to take on a fluffier, more dense form, and is available under such reputed brand names as Eco Earth and Bed-a-Beast.

10. Your   ideal substrate should have no traces of fertilizers,   chemical   formulations,   pesticides, insecticides, manure or vermiculite.

11. The substrate may also contain some top-soil content free of additives and chemicals, but it should be packed in loosely. It is also important that the top-soil never become too wet, and if it does dampen, is extracted and replaced from the tank at the earliest.

12. Substrates that may be acidic in nature, with a pH level of 3.5 or even lower should be avoided completely. Alkaline substrates are what are ideal for the sensitive moist skins of the Tiger Salamanders and acidic substrates made of such components as peat moss will cause dehydration and an irregularity in the caudate

electrolyte equilibrium. This could accelerate into such ailments as toxicity, infection and even death.

13. Elements such as gravel must most certainly not be incorporated as they be may easily ingested the Tiger Salamander and cause choking hazards, among other ailments. If you must have some kind of stone layer for drainage of fecal and food matter, and for an aesthetic appeal, opt for broad, flat stones with a smooth surface. Place these stones at lower levels that are harder to access. It is best if these stones are used to cement in potted plants to the vivarium floor.

14. Certain woods should never be allowed into the vivarium, such as drifting twigs or barks from pine or cedar. The oils emitted by these trees are too chemically potent for the delicate skin of the Tiger Salamander and may cause toxicity upon reaction with the caudate skin.

15. Lastly, the ideal substrate will incorporate plenty of hiding spots for the Tiger Salamanders to wander about in. They will also need tunnels, whether by their own design, or already fitted in by another creature. The tunnels, especially are needed as Tiger Salamanders like to emerge from these spaces and consider the resultant surface their home. This practice is useful to you as a new owner introducing the pet to the vivarium for the first time.

16. You can easily erect makeshift tunnels for the Salamander to pass through, made out of such materials as flimsy bamboo sheets and PVC pipes. The tunnels should be inserted into the ground with the end angling outward into the vivarium. The Tiger salamander, when placed in form the opposite end,

should journey through the tunnel and end up within the confines of the vivarium.

3.   Regulating the Temperature

The right temperature in the vivarium makes a lot of difference to the survival and wellbeing of your Tiger Salamander. In general, these caudates exist comfortable in temperatures that range between 65 and 75 degrees Fahrenheit, or 18 and 21 degrees Celsius. Being hardy by nature, their bodies can also adapt easily to a shift of two or three degrees in temperature in either direction. However, it is essential that the temperature of the vivarium itself be consistently maintained, so as not to stress the Tiger Salamanders.

In captivity, Tiger Salamanders have been observed to better at lower temperatures than higher ones. This could be due to their preference for the cooler and moist conditions of tunnels and burrows below the earth's surface. While you may maintain the temperature of your vivarium at towards the higher end of their tolerance spectrum, bear in mind that this temperature does not exceed a limit of 78 degrees Fahrenheit, or 25.5 degrees Celsius, after adjusting for a shift to a warmer temperature. When exposed to high bouts of heat for an extended period of time, Tiger Salamanders come under distress, experience dehydration of skin and may then develop other ailments as a result. It is best to place a thermometer attached to the vivarium so you can accurately monitor the environment within the vivarium, instead of having to guess how cool or warm it is.

If you live in cooler climates, and find that you need to provide additional heating to the tank, it is best to do so using heating pads. These pads, when placed under the surface of the tank, can raise the temperature gently without any harmful exposure caused to the caudates by such sources as heating lamps or basking lamps. The heating pad should preferably be placed at the corner of the tank, covering a third of the surface at maximum, to allow a cooler surface area for burrowing, should the caudates require it.

Tiger Salamanders rely largely on the moisture in their environment to provide them with hydration. For these purposes, it becomes your responsibility to ensure that the vivarium never becomes too dry. From the substrate to the air circulating within, every aspect of the vivarium should serve to provide an adequate amount of moisture to the Tiger salamander's skin. This can be achieved by placing a small shallow bowl of water in the corner of the tank, and allowing for a coco-husk substrate to collect and absorb moisture that is released into the atmosphere.

Sufficient ventilation is also essential to the maintenance of a healthily-regulated atmosphere within the tank. It is essential that clean oxygen be allowed to enter the vivarium in a constant flow, without giving the caudates a chance to slip out of their homes. You can accomplish this by covering the top of the tank with a wire mesh fitting. A poorly-ventilated vivarium may not only become over-heated, but will also become moist and damp, becoming a hotspot for disease and infections.

4.   Providing ideal Lighting conditions

Lighting does not play as big of a role as the other factors that go into setting up the ideal vivarium for your Tiger Salamander. Most of the benefits that natural light can give your Tiger Salamanders, such as Vitamin D, can be received through a smart and regulated diet of live feed and supplements. In addition, Tiger salamanders are nocturnal creatures that prefer the dark hours to the light times of the day.

Most forms of conventional lighting also impart some amount of heat, which will make a difference to the overall temperature of the tank. If the temperature of the vivarium is already swinging towards the heavier side of the pendulum, any further heat from the lighting may only cause stress to the night-loving Tiger Salamanders.

However, should you house any live plants in the vivarium along with the Tiger Salamanders; some form of lighting then becomes essential. Without any source of light, the plants in the tank will be unable to process food and will subsequently die. The key is to find a lighting source that can sustain plant life in the vivarium without putting the caudates under any distress.

The best lighting for this purpose has been found to be UVB lighting fixtures, preferable low-wattage fluorescent tubes. This form of lighting manages to impart light that is absorbed by the plants without emitting any extra heat. In addition, UVB lighting does not illuminate the entire space, leaving Tiger Salamanders with darker areas, should they feel uncomfortable with the light. It is best to place the lights in a corner at an angle, rather than fix them flat and center at the roof of the tank. This setting will further create dark spots for the ease and comfort of your pets.
The nature of the lighting should also mimic the daily cycle of the Tiger Salamanders. The caudate usually spends

about 12 hours in the dark, burrowed underground, and the rest of its time wandering lazily on the surface. Try to regulate the lighting to be on when the caudate needs it, and off when your pet is ready to rest. The best kind of lighting options that encourage this kind of setting are ambient light fixtures with minimal heat emissions. Heavier lighting options, such as Full spectrum lighting, may flood the enclosure with too much light and stress your pets out.

If you do have lighting fixtures in the enclosure that affect the heating of the vivarium, it is best to regulate the temperature to accommodate this change. If you live in an area that has a climate of 65 to 75 degrees Fahrenheit for a better part of the year, the temperature in the vivarium should be hospitable enough, even with the addition of lighting.

If you live in cooler climates and feel the need to provide additional heating than the light can emit, consider using a heating pad that is tucked away under the tank at the very corner, so as not to overheat the bottom. It is also essential that you keep a constant watch on temperature, lest it become too hot and cause your pets distress.

For the most part, UVB lighting has been observed to be effective and have little adverse effects on the health of the Tiger Salamanders. Some studies and observations have even shown that overexposure to UVB lighting sources like sun lamps, black lights and even direct sunrays have caused damage to the eyes and skin of some caudates. It is for this reason that, if necessary, the UVB lighting be of a low fluorescent quality, along with being regulated to be shut for at least 10 hours a day. It is also best that you keep your caudates away from direct sunlight, and house the vivarium in quiet, dark and shady area of your house.

5.   Assessing the Water requirements of the Tank

Whether they remain aquatic neotenic, or make the more common transition to terrestrial inhabitants, Tiger Salamanders, like all amphibians, require a body of water in their premises in order for them to survive. As caudates who absorb hydration and moisture through their pores instead of drinking with their mouths, a constant source of water becomes doubly essential to keep them thriving.

No matter how much of your vivarium surface is taken up by water, ensure that it is as clean and fresh as possible. Most Tiger Salamanders adapt perfectly well to regular tap water, kept at room temperature, provided that the water is free of any traces of chlorine. Chlorine has been studied to be extremely toxic to the delicate systems of Tiger Salamanders, and in combination with other chemicals in tap water, may become potentially lethal.

Tiger Salamander breeders and owners have mostly noticed that fresh rainwater also seems to be well-suited for a vivarium, provided this water has not been stagnant before collection. Stagnant rainwater is a breeding hotspot for germs, bacteria and viruses, and is unadvisable as an addition to your tank. You may think to use distilled water, but this also an unwise option. Distilled water is usually over-treated, to a point where it is stripped off essential minerals that the Tiger Salamanders will need. Bottled spring water is an ideal choice, but is too expensive an option to consider for most potential owners.

If it is difficult or inconvenient for you to provide rainwater for your tank, you can undertake a simple de-chlorination process by treating your water with a water conditioner.

These inexpensive conditioners are easily available at most local pet stores and markets, and are efficient at cleaning away traces of chlorine, a related particle known as chloramine, as well as any heavy metals.

If you are raising solely adult Tiger Salamanders, you will not even need to place a very large source of water within the vivarium. Along with the water body, Tiger Salamanders also absorb moisture through the air in the atmosphere, and the water content of their prey. If you must, place a small and shallow bowl of clean water tucked away at a corner of the vivarium. Placing the bowl away from the hub of activity is also important as Tiger Salamanders tend to use the water as a spot for shedding excrement. If placed in the centre of the vivarium, the fecal matter could pollute the environment in no time.

To ensure that the water provided to your Tiger Salamanders, even if in a small bowl, is healthy and fresh, change it at least once daily. If you are housing larvae or neotene, you may take longer breaks between switching the water contents, but ensure that you switch the water in an aquatic space at least once a week for best results. Adult Tiger Salamanders do not transition into the strongest of swimmers, so their water bowl should not be deep. The curious Tiger Salamander may wander into the bowl, become trapped, and if left unnoticed, may eventually drown.

6.   Cleaning and Maintaining the Vivarium

You may take care to provide the best housing conditions for your Tiger Salamanders, but if you are not able to clean and maintain the environment in a disciplined and committed manner, you definitely will end up putting the health and well-being of your Tiger Salamanders at risk. Here are a few tips to ensure that your vivarium is taken care of in the best way possible:

1. Always take the time to conduct a daily inspection and cleaning of the tank, as the Tiger Salamanders will constantly cloud their environment with fecal matter, food remains and skin that was shed but not eaten.

2. The water should be cleaned and changed once in a week or two, with all of the elements and accessories taken out.

3.   The Tiger Salamanders should be taken out the tank and placed in a separate sterilized tank until the cleaning is complete.

4.   The tank should then be sterilized with the help of an amphibian-safe disinfectant.

5.   Clean and wipe all the accessories and decorative elements of the tank, disinfecting those as necessary.

6.   Before you transfer the Tiger Salamander back into the vivarium, give the tank a final rinse with de chlorinated tap water and then place back all the elements to complete your maintenance.

7.   It is important that you maintain a moist substrate for the survival   and   thriving   of   your   Tiger Salamanders. You can mist the vivarium about once a day or every two days if it is required, but ensure that you do not make the atmosphere too damp, lest it breed bacteria and fungi.

8.   You will also need to change the substrate itself every two to three weeks. This is important as the old substrate will, at one point, have no more room for moisture absorption. It may also have become too dirty and cannot be kept in the tank without the risk of contaminating the environment.

9.   A good way of telling that it is time to change your substrate is when the tank begins emitting a faint yet rank odor. If left unattended, this damp smell may

become more intense, signaling the rotting and decomposing of your substrate.

10. You may also notice tiny black gnats taking birth and wandering around the tank in an old substrate. If this happens, your substrate has already become too aged and needs to be changed at once to prevent parasitic ailments to the Tiger Salamanders

Chapter Seven: Feeding your Tiger Salamander

Tiger Salamanders are not pets who require a social environment, or any kind of company besides a mate during the breeding season. To further cement their need for isolation, the caudates have skin that is extremely reactive to even the most basic natural salts and oils on your skin. This limits any interaction you many have with your Tiger Salamander, save for feeding times. It is perhaps because of this rare opportunity to bond with the Tiger Salamander that most owners tend to enjoy mealtimes with their smiling amphibian pets.

Another reason that may add to the fun during mealtimes with your Tiger salamander is that they tend to have generous appetites, and will show great excitement when you arrive with the food. Once they recognize you as the food provider , they will, in fact, start looking forward to mealtimes, eagerly reaching for food as you drop it in.

1.   What to Feed your Tiger Salamander

Thanks to the voracious appetite of your Tiger salamanders, they will happily gobble up just about any kind of food you provide them, provided it is small enough, looks delicious to them and wriggles about. This gives you a wide array of feeding opportunities with which to make mealtimes enriching and interesting for them.

Among the most nutritious and easily available foods to provide your pets with are crickets, earthworms, superworms, wax worms, night crawlers and cockroaches.

Worms are, in fact, the most popular choice of live feed for Tiger Salamanders, due to a variety of reasons.

To begin with, these wriggly creatures are small enough and soft enough to be digested by the younger Tiger Salamander larvae, but wriggly enough to stimulate foraging habits when dropped into an adult's tank. In addition all types of worms, particularly red worms and earthworms, are highly nutritious and readily accepted by the caudates. These easy-to-handle forms of feed can also be purchased easily, even cultured at home inexpensively, and are excellent for long-term storage.

Crickets are another highly popular choice of food for Tiger Salamanders. While a little more challenging to feed to your caudates, and also less nutritionally dense than worms or other forms of live feed, the caudates seem to show a preference for these creatures.

Crickets contain very low levels of calcium, a mineral essential for the growth and development of Tiger Salamanders. In addition, live crickets, when lowered into the tank, may even try to bite or attack your pets, although this seems to a challenge the caudates enjoy! Do not leave the crickets, if uneaten, in the tank for too long. The small nips may then turn into prolonged fierce attacks that will harm the Tiger Salamander's skin.

Tiger Salamanders are carnivorous by nature, and will enjoy nearly any type of live feed that you can provide. In their natural habitat, these caudates rely on an array of food sources to prey on. Giving them a diet that consists of more than just worms and crickets will prevent them from becoming bored and listless at mealtimes, and will also give you the chance to try out more nutritionally potent food options. Try such forms of live feed as grasshoppers, moths, woodlice, flour beetles and caterpillars.

When you provide live feed to the younger Tiger Salamander larvae, you will have to be mindful that the food is soft and small enough to fit into their mouths comfortably. As the larvae develop, however, their demand for bigger, hardier food will increase, and it is important that you keep up with this wish. With a healthy appetite that develops very early, Tiger salamander larvae will often resort to feeding on each other if they feel that their requirements aren't being met.

Adult Tiger Salamanders can handle more solid and complex forms of food. In fact, dropping in live insects at mealtimes may also become a form of entertainment for you, as Tiger Salamanders are eager foragers. Unlike other varieties of salamanders, and even such amphibians as frogs, Tiger Salamanders are not lazy, shy though they may be. They enjoy the act of hunting, killing and consuming their food. With a unique set of movements and hunting patterns, you will truly witness a mini-spectacle come feeding time.

Carnivorous though they may be, it does not open up just about any type of meat for their feeding. Mammalian meat such as beef, pork or the like, for instance, may be nutritionally dense, but may also be too complex for the caudates to digest, and contain levels of fat that will encourage obesity. Seafood such as shrimp, crustacean or fish are similarly not quite suitable for Tiger Salamanders, in addition to some having too high a salt content.

A certain type of mammalian meat, in the form of pink mice, is sometimes fed to the Tiger Salamanders, the emphasis being on the word "sometimes". While again being a high source of nutrition for the Tiger Salamanders, these mammals must be fed live and are prone to attacking their hunters. When given as a rare treat, about once a month or even less frequently, however, these mice could be a meal to look forward to.

And the meat of other amphibians is a strict no-no. One of your main endeavors, from the Tiger Salamander's childhood, is to raise it to be non-cannibalistic. By encouraging it to feed on its kind, you stimulate the unnecessary act of turning on its own kind, making it essential for the caudate to be housed in isolation thereafter.

It is important to know that the adult Tiger Salamanders prefer live feed that they can scavenge for and personally "hunt down". Moving prey triggers their foraging instincts, making mealtimes an engaging experience for you and the pet. Larvae only require food to be of the right size and consistency: living or dead does not affect their appetite. Therefore, you will have to personally deposit food into the tank at mealtimes.

Tiger Salamander larvae will accept non-live feed, even in frozen form. This feed can easily be scooped up with your fingers, a pair of pincers or a small spoon and placed into the tank. Some larvae may even accept commercially-prepared pellets and flakes – consult with your local exotic pet expert to find the best brands for you. For the adults, however, live feed – specifically those that aren't pellets or flakes – are the feed of choice. As they may reject food that has been severed and chopped up, you can either use your bare hands, or even a pair of pincers or tweezers, to deposit the prey into the vivarium. The Tiger Salamander will either scoop the prey out of the grasp of your fingers or tweezers, or allow it to fall to the floor and commence "hunting" it down.

You can then spend the next few minutes watching your pet chase down its prey, grasp it by the neck, snap it neatly and then proceed to swallow it. Tiger Salamanders do not generally appear to chew their food, and you will therefore witness the regular spectacle of feed being consumed whole. This is especially fascinating to watch when a slimy worm is slurped up by a hungry caudate, or when a considerably large night crawler struggles valiantly as he is gobbled up by the Tiger Salamander over a leisurely period of a few minutes.

As a means to enable the digestion of food swallowed up whole, Tiger salamanders may often exhibit abrupt facial and body twitches. You may notice the caudate suddenly squeeze its eyes closed, or look around lazily with its mouth opening in a yawn. This movement that mimics yawning, is, in fact, the Tiger Salamander's way of aiding the food down the digestive tract and into the stomach for further breaking down and adsorption.

2. Tips on nutritionally-dense live feed for your Tiger Salamander

Wholly carnivorous by nature, Tiger Salamanders have very few requirements for the meats around them to qualify as edible. If the prey in front of them is smaller in size, has a neck that can be snapped easily and most importantly, is alive, then the adult Tiger Salamander is more than willing to hunt it down and consume it.

In fact, their natural foraging and scavenging behaviour is triggered by the frantic movement of creatures when they are hungry, be it a bug, caterpillar, cricket or even another Tiger Salamander. The preference for live feed over commercially manufactured or frozen feed is mostly shown by the adult Tiger Salamanders. The larvae, on the other hand, are not too concerned with the life state of the feed, so long as it is small and easily digested.

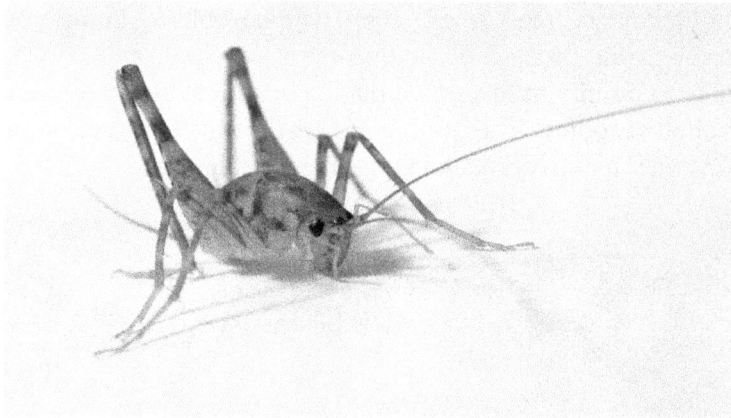

Because Tiger Salamanders are not too fussy when it comes to food, it can be easy for you, as a caregiver, to supply them whatever is easy to procure, feed and store. Different types of worms, along with crickets are among the easiest food sources to find, and are also readily accepted by the caudates. Due to convenience, you may ignore other types of live feed that could sustain your Tiger Salamander; this, however, will adversely affect your pet's health.

Delectable to the caudate though they may be, popular worms such as red worms and crickets are not as nutritionally valuable to your pets. Your Tiger Salamanders require food that is rich in such minerals as calcium and phosphorus for the development and maintenance of their skin and colouring, along with their bones. The feed your pets receive should also be rich in carotene, a substance that aids the developing of colour pigmentation on the Tiger Salamanders' bodies.

With a little education and research, you can easily compile a healthy list of foods that will add flavour as well as nourishment to the Tiger Salamanders' palate. Your exotic pet expert is a good source to receive information on the right kind of feed from. They will be able to guide you through the process of finding the right food, and also be able to point you towards reliable pet stores, bait shops and online resources. To further help you out; here are some tips on which food pack in a nutritional punch:

• Foods that are ideal for the Tiger Salamander are those that are not only rich in calcium and phosphorus, but also contain these minerals in the right proportion. Earthworms and nightcrawlers are considered "perfect" in terms of nutritional value, as well as taste for your Tiger Salamanders.

• Red wiggler worms are also considered to be nutritionally potent are ideal as part of your Tiger Salamander's diet. Be careful when handling these worms, however; when chopped up, the worms exude a vile smell. This odor usually repels Tiger Salamanders, but curiously, is not emitted when the worm is left whole. Therefore, red worms are best suited as whole live bait for adult Tiger Salamanders.

• Crickets are a favorite meal among Tiger Salamanders; they are also among the least nutritious. While filled with other nutrients, crickets have a very low calcium-phosphorus rate, making them unsuitable as the predominant form of feed. A diet that only provides crickets to the caudates will lead their bones and skin to slowly atrophy and develop ailments. Foods such as crickets, are ideally "enhanced" with nutrients using methods such as gut-loading or supplement dusting.

• Foods such as wax worms and pinky or fuzzy mice are another favorite food of the Tiger Salamanders, and not surprisingly so. These foods, while being alarmingly low in their calcium-phosphorus ratio, do have a high fat content, enjoyed by the Tiger Salamanders. While a tasty treat handed to your pet once in a rare while, do not make a habit of overfeeding wax worms and pinky worms to the caudates. They will most likely gobble up every morsel greedily, and develop obesity-related issues at a rapid rate.

• It seems that most worms, besides the humble earthworm, are unsuitable for the Tiger Salamander; this is not so. If you can find the phoenix worm in your area, or even source it through the Internet, you have hit the Tiger Salamander diet jackpot. Not only are phoenix worms loaded with the right proportion of nutrients needed by the caudate, but also contain the right amount of fat, with minimal risks of obesity to the caudates.

3. Maximizing the Mineral Intake in Tiger Salamander Feed

As we have already discussed, many of the insects that you will feed your Tiger Salamander are low in essential calcium and phosphorus levels. It is difficult to find foods that contain the idle calcium-phosphorus ratio, and your Tiger Salamander cannot subsist on such foods as phoenix worms alone.

Many Tiger salamander owners, therefore, supplement the feed they provide to the Tiger Salamanders, both larvae and adult, with additional nutrient formulations. These formulations are easily available at most exotic pet stores and even online. Your exotic pet expert should be able to guide you towards a trusted brand for your Tiger Salamander. Once prepared, these formulations are imparted to the live feed using one of two methods: gut loading and supplement dusting.

Gut loading the Tiger Salamander's Feed

Gut loading is a relatively simple way to ensure that live feed such as crickets are nutritious enough for the Tiger Salamanders; to do so, however requires an act that will passively begin killing the crickets even before they reach your caudates.

The process of gut loading basically comprises of preparing a diet comprising of the calcium-phosphorus formulation for the crickets, and administering it to them around 48 hours before feeding to the caudates. A lethal adversity to calcium is a major reason for the low content of this mineral in the crickets' bodies. Once ingested, therefore, the calcium will slowly start to kill the crickets, even while making its way out through the digestive process.

Your next step is to feed the the crickets to the Tiger salamanders, ideally as soon as the 48 hour mark is up and even slightly earlier, if possible. You require over a day after feeding the crickets to allow the breakdown and absorption of calcium into the system. Remember, however, that a little calcium is enough to kill the cricket, and the excess is then thrown out through the excrement.

If the crickets die before they reach the Tiger Salamanders, the caudates may reject this non-living form of bait. Furthermore, if the crickets do excrete before they make it to the caudates, then the calcium content will be lost through the feces, rendering your attempts futile. Ideally, the crickets should be eaten within a couple of hours of depositing to your pet caudates, with any leftover cleared away at the earliest.

Supplement dusting the Tiger Salamander's feed

As simple as the process of gut loading may be, it also comes with a high risk of failure, in addition to being time-consuming. You may not always have the requisite 48 hours to feed the crickets and wait for their slow doom; sometimes, you may not have the heart. In these cases, it helps to use the other option available to enhance your Tiger Salamander's feed: supplement dusting.

This extremely simple method requires you to do nothing more than purchase the right nutrient supplement formulations and dust them onto the live feed. According to many exotic pet experts and Tiger Salamander owners, such brands as Rep Cal Calcium with Vitamin D3 and Herptivite are highly recommended as being nutritionally complete. Easy to use and store, the only precaution you have to take is to ensure that containers are replaced within six months of opening, as they may lose nutritional value.

The advantage that supplement dusting has over gut loading is the immediacy of its use. You will dust the powder onto the crickets or similar insects just before feeding them to your Tiger Salamanders. A common way to effectively coat your crickets with a liberal amount of dust is to place the crickets in a ziploc bag, pour a generous amount of formulation over the crickets, seal the ziploc bag and then shake it vigorously. Now, open the bag and pluck out the dusted crickets to place in the tank.

You will also have to ensure that the Tiger Salamanders consumer the dusted crickets as quickly as possible. Since the supplements have only been added externally and in a light manner, the formulation will begin to trickle off the crickets as soon as it begins moving about. Ideally, Tiger Salamander feed is dusted with supplements about once every week, to ensure a steady but not overzealous supply of nutrition. Since the Tiger salamander larvae develop at a faster rate, they may require more nutrients and a more frequent supplement during of their feed; about once every two or three days should suffice.

4.   Frequency of the Feed and Successful Feeding Habits

Tiger Salamanders are creatures of summertime foraging and wintertime estivation. Their appetites and the frequency of the feeding seems to be largely reliant on the temperatures in their surroundings. Warmer climates have been observed to open up their appetites, while cooler temperatures cause them to want food less frequently, instead preferring to shut down and rest. Bearing this rule of thumb in mind, you will generally feed your Tiger Salamanders more frequently in the summer months than in the winter.

In case you maintain a regulated temperature, the frequency of the feed will then depend on the which end of the temperature spectrum your set temperature falls on. In an ideal setting with the temperature of the vivarium ranging between 60 and 72 degrees Fahrenheit, adult Tiger Salamanders should be fed once every two to three days. If the temperature of the vivarium falls towards the higher end, i.e. 72 degrees Fahrenheit, then a meal every couple of days is essential. If, on the other hand, the temperature falls towards the lower end at 60 degrees Fahrenheit, then providing food to the adult Tiger Salamanders even once a week should meet their dietary requirements. The caudates themselves have been observed to exhibit decreased senses of appetite during the cooler months, regardless of the temperature of the vivarium.

Larval Tiger Salamanders, on the other hand, will need to be fed about once every two days initially, and then perhaps even once daily as they approach metamorphosis. Once they make the transition into adulthood, their appetites should match those of the other adults, and you can time your meals based on the amount they consume in one session.

The frequency of your feed also matters to the general environment of the vivarium; any extra food left in the substrate will begin to decay and contaminate the surroundings. Figuring out how much your pet need in one mealtime, and allowing it just that much food will help keep the vivarium as clean possible. You can determine how much your adult Tiger will need per feeding simply by observing how much it eats in one sitting.

Some Tiger Salamander owners like to feed their pets using their fingers to pluck and deposit food into the tank. When fed this way, the Tiger salamander tends to eat at a slightly quicker rate, consuming enough food in an approximate period of ten minutes. If you are queasy about handling feed with your fingers or even tweezers, you can place food for your Tiger Salamanders in a small dish and deposit the dish into the tank. The feed can then wander about and stimulate foraging habits in the caudates. Observe how actively the Tiger Salamanders pursue and they consume their prey, before ignoring the remaining food. On an average, an adult Tiger Salamander should accept about 3-4 worms or insects in one feed; any more constitutes overfeeding.

If you like to entice your Tiger Salamanders with their food in order to give them some activity and exercise, you can use a piece of debris from the tank, such as a small twig or log instead of your fingers and hand tweezers, and place the food on it. Then, wave the debris close to the Tiger Salamander, forcing it leap at the food or chase after it.

Some Tiger Salamander owners like to move their pets to a separate environment for feeding and foraging. This is usually an especially constructed habitat that allows the adult caudates to feed at their will and convenience. After they are done, the owners then transfer them back into their original vivarium. This practice is considered convenient for those who do not like to dirty the vivarium with leftover food debris and cause potential ailments among the pets.

Know, however, that it is not a necessary practice. While a good precaution to take against illness, you can also ensure the wellbeing of your Tiger Salamander by simply being disciplined in your tank cleaning and maintenance habits. Furthermore, shifting the Tiger Salamanders from one tank to another constantly may agitate them, cause them unnecessary stress and may even injure them in the process.

As long as you remember to clear away fecal matter and food debris a few hours after every feed, and change the water on a regular basis, your environment should be healthy enough to house your Tiger Salamanders for feeding as well as wandering and resting. It is preferable that you feed the caudates at night, in order to complement their feeding routines in the wild. It is also essential that you maintain a regular frequency of supplementing your Tiger Salamanders feed with the necessary nutritional formulations.

5.   List of Foods that can be Fed to your Tiger Salamanders

Name	Value of feed	Benefits of feed	Draw-backs of feed	Best sources of feed

Night Crawlers Lobe Worms	Excellent	Highly nutritious Easily available Accepted by pets Suitable for aquatic and land-breathers	Must be cut up for younger pets	Bait shops Gardens, backyards, Discount stores Online traders
Live Black Worms (*Lumbri culus variegat us*)	Excellent	Highly nutritious Accepted by smaller pets Does not grow into insect	Not for adult terrestrial Tiger Salamanders	Pet stores (United States, Australia) Online traders
Live Blood-worms (*Chirono mus spp.*)	Excellent	Highly nutritious Accepted by smaller, aquatic pets	Not for adult terrestrial Tiger Salamanders Will develop into flies May grow in infested waters May cause	Some pet stores in Europe and Asia Rarely found in United States

			allergies to humans	Online traders
Live Tubifex Worms	Excellent	Highly nutritious Accepted by smaller, aquatic pets Does not grow into insect	Not for adult terrestrial Tiger Salamanders May grow in infested waters	Some pet stores in Europe and Asia Rarely found in United States Online traders
Daphnia and Scuds	Excellent	Highly nutritious Accepted by smaller, aquatic pets Rich in Carotene Good feed for larvae	Not for adult terrestrial Tiger Salamanders Need regular culture for supply purposes Not easily available	Some pet stores Online traders Hunting/her ping

White Worms	Good	Highly nutritious Accepted by smaller, aquatic pets	Not for adult terrestrial Tiger Salamanders Need regular culture for supply purposes Poor source of carotene	Live food culture Home culture Other feed dealers
Wax Worms	Good	Good source of nutrition Accepted by most terrestrial, some aquatic Tiger Salamanders	Unsuitable for small Tiger Salamanders Unsuitable as staple diet Very high in calories and fats	Some pet stores Online traders
Live Grubs	Excellent	Highly nutritious Available in sizes Suitable for aquatic and land-breathers	Uneaten grubs may hatch and grow Not widely available	Some pet stores Online traders

Live Wild "Bugs"	Excellent to Fair	Highly nutritious Available in sizes Suitable for aquatic and land-breathers	Some varieties may not be accepted Difficult to catch May escape or grow Risk of bringing pests into home Risk of bringing chemicals into home	Caught fro m the wild
Live Crickets	Good	Easily available	Difficult to catch Uneaten crickets may bite pets Unsuitable for aquatic breathers Poor Calcium phosphorus ratio	Pet stores Online tra ders
Fruit Flies	Good	Suitable for smaller terrestrial breathers Easy to culture at home	Unsuitable for aquatic and larger Tiger Salamanders inadequate supply of calcium	Pet stores Online trade Home culture

Frozen Worms	Good	Adequate nutrition Easy to store Suitable for aquatic breathers Easily available	Unsuitable for terrestrial and larger Tiger Salamanders some varieties may slime up water Lack of movement does not stimulate feeding	
Red Wigglers	Good	Good nutritional value Relatively easily available	May emit foul secretion on cutting and be rejected by pet	Bait shops Pet stores online trade
Live Brine Shrimp (Artemia)	Good	Good nutritional value Eggs easy to procure Adults easily available at stores	Unsuitable for medium, large or terrestrial Tiger Salamanders only fed after eggs hatch High amounts of salt	Pet stores online trade

Live Mealworms	Fair	Easily available Wriggling stimulates feeding response from pets	Hard-to-digest exoskeleton High in fat content May bite Tiger Salamanders	Pet stores online trade
Canned and Wet-Pack Foods	Fair	Easily available Simple to use and store	May be rejected by Tiger Salamanders	Pet stores
Freeze Dried Worms	Fair	Easily available	Rejected as feed by many Tiger Salamanders Unsuitable for larger or terrestrial Tiger Salamanders Less nutrition value than live or frozen varieties	Pet stores

Frozen Brine Shrimp	Fair	Easily available Can be stored in freezer	Rejected as feed by many Tiger Salamanders Unsuitable for larger or terrestrial Tiger Salamander Less nutritional value than live varieties Contains high amounts of salt	Pet stores
Meat and Organ Meat	Fair	Easily available Can be stored in freezer	Rejected by many Tiger Salamanders Unnatural source of feed for Tiger Salamanders low calcium and vitamin content excess Vitamin A (liver) may cause hypervitaminos is energy dense and may cause obesity	Pet stores Meat vendors and markets

Raw Fish and Shrimp	Good to Fair	Easily avai lable Can be stored in freezer high protein levels Low fat levels	Rejected by many Tiger Salamanders Unnatural source of feed for Tiger Salamander low calcium and vitamin content in some types excess levels of salt in some types	Pet stores Fish/ seafood vendors and markets
Feeder Fish	Poor	Easily available	Low thiamine levels in some type Low fatty acid content in some types may cause obesity unsuitable for smaller or terrestrial Tiger Salamanders possible disease carrier.trigger too fast for most Tiger Salamanders to catch	Pet stores

Mice and Other Rodents	Poor	Easily available rich in nutritional value	Unnatural source of feed for Tiger Salamander Only suitable for larger Tiger Salamanders energy dense and may cause obesity may bite Tiger Salamanders	Pet stores
Freeze Dried Brine Shrimp and Krill	Poor	Easily available	Unsuitable for larger Tiger Salamanders High levels of salt Less nutrition that frozen or live varieties	Pet stores
Freeze Dried Crickets and Mealworms	Poor	Easily available	Unsuitable for smaller and terrestrial Tiger Salamanders Rejected by most Tiger Salamanders Almost devoid of nutritional value Messy to feed and clean	Pet stores

Pellets	Good to Poor	Easily available Simple to use and store Complete in nutritional value	Some varieties unsuitable for Tiger Salamanders Unsuitable for terrestrial Tiger Salamanders Contents include wheat,corn, artificial food sources Leftover pellets may make water cloudy	Pet stores online trader
Fish Flakes	Poor	Easily available Simple to use and store	Some varieties unsuitable for Tiger Salamanders Unsuitable for terrestrial Tiger Salamanders Contents include wheat, corn, artificial food sources Leftover flakes may make water cloudy	Pet stores

Other Amphibi-ans	Inapprop-riate	Very high in nutrition value	Potentially toxic food source possible carrier/trigger of disease may injure Tiger Salamanders	Pet stores Sourced from wild

Chapter Eight: Interacting with your Tiger Salamander

As pets, Tiger Salamanders are generously hardy and adaptable, will learn to eagerly accept food from their caregivers and will provide their owners will a well-lived companionship that may last over two decades. During this time, you will obviously want to, and need to, physically interact with your pet. It is important to understand, however, that interacting with a Tiger Salamander is largely different from interacting with a mammalian or aviary pet.

Tiger Salamanders like to live their days in isolation and are shy and underground-friendly creatures by nature. While they will not need for you to pet them on a regular basis, they will soon come to recognize you as their feeder and caregiver. This will lead to them greeting you eagerly at mealtimes, often by scurrying quickly to the front of the tank. When you lower food into the vivarium, you may feel the odd nip from your caudate pet, although this is just an eager response to the prey they intend to consume. For all we know about the mysterious smiling caudates, this nip may even be an affectionate way of greeting their caregivers!

Apart from mealtimes, you will only interact with your Tiger Salamander while cleaning the tank or administering medical treatments. This is not only advisable, but essentially a necessity, due to the highly sensitive nature of the Tiger Salamander's skin. Through this chapter you will understand how the right type of handling affects your interaction with the Tiger Salamander and also its health. You will also receive an insight into the interpersonal dynamics that Tiger Salamanders may share, when housed together.

1.   Handling your Tiger Salamander

If you have owned a mammalian or even aviary pet or even some reptiles, your interactions with them would have consisted of several tangible moments. From picking, to stroking, petting, even cuddling your pets, how we physically handle our pets conveys plenty of emotion and care. Your nurturing emotions for your Tiger Salamander, however, cannot be as tactile in their expression.

To understand the importance of handling your caudate the right way, it helps to know a little about the value of their skin in their daily lives. Tiger Salamanders have an outer layer of dermis that is extremely flimsy and sensitive to the touch. This flimsy texture not only helps the caudate shed its exterior with relative ease every few weeks, but also helps it absorb moisture and hydration.

In fact, some amphibians, such as woodland salamanders and red backed salamanders rely on the pores of their skin to provide them with hydration, as well as oxygen. Our own Tiger Salamander friends themselves absorb abundant amounts of oxygen through the pores on their skin, along with the roof and lining of their mouths. To enable such absorption, the pores have to be open, relatively large and welcoming to external elements.

Human bodies, on the other hand, use the pores on their skin not only as a form of absorption, but also excretion. The surfaces of our hands are constantly coated with a thin layer of naturally secreted oils as well as salt from residual sweat. While relatively harmless to us and many other species, these natural oils and salts tend to have exaggerated adverse effects on the Tiger Salamander's skin. Upon contact, the natural secretions from our hands cause the pores of the caudate to dry out, even become clogged. Human bodies, on the other hand, use the pores on their skin not only as a form of absorption, but also excretion. The surfaces of our hands are constantly coated with a thin layer of naturally secreted oils as well as salt from residual sweat.

While relatively harmless to us and many other species, these natural oils and salts tend to have exaggerated adverse effects on the Tiger Salamander's skin. Upon contact, the natural secretions from our hands cause the pores of the caudate to dry out, even become clogged.

This makes it difficult for the Salamander to receive hydration and may make the animal lethargic, drowsy and eventually ill. In the case of such amphibians as woodland salamanders, the reaction their pores have to human skin is so acute that simply picking them up with bare hands could cause the oxygen supply to be blocked and result in their death.

It is for these reasons that it becomes essential to pick up and handle your pet caudate the right way. And you will need to physically handle the harp on a regular basis, more so when it's time to clean out its tank, transport it or give it a medical examination. Do not let the worry of "poisoning" your pet's skins with natural oils make you anxious about handling it, though. With the right preparatory steps and tools in hand, you can swiftly and safely usher your caudate about, without causing stress to the pet or yourself. Here are step-by-step directions on how to handle your Tiger Salamander the proper way.

1. To start off, you will need hands that are clean, not only of sweats, salts and oils, but also of any chemically-formulated products, such as perfumes, sprays, cosmetics, lotions, etc. Such formulations are toxic for your pet, and may lead to potentially life-threatening ailments.

2. If you do have any such products applied, wash your hands clean with a disinfectant, scrubbing thoroughly and vigorously.

3. Pat your hands dry, and then wet them again with plain water. This will ensure that your hands are free of any soapy residue.

4. Do not dry your hands, as you will need a watery buffer to safeguard the Tiger Salamander's skin from your own.

5. Then, lower your hand and gently, yet firmly, pick up your Tiger Salamander, with your fingers clasping its body between both pairs of legs.

6. As soon as it is picked up, your caudate may start to wriggle about. This occurs and the Tiger Salamander feels unsure of an environment in which its feet are suspended with no floor for support. You can ease your pet and help it stay calm by placing the palm of your other hand below its feet, creating a false floor.

7. You may need to examine your pet's body on a regular basis, from the underside to the ends and even the limbs – tricky to do when both your hands are supporting the Tiger Salamander. To examine your pet, hold the index finger of your free hand out and place the caudate at the top tip, letting its body run down the length of your finger.

8. The finger also acts as a fake floor for your pet's feet. To secure its body from wriggling as you examine, gently cover the Tiger Salamander's body with your thumb.

9. Nestled safely between both fingers, the caudate should remain still while you check them.

10. To release the caudate, simply lower your hand back into the vivarium and release your grip. The Tiger Salamander will quickly scurry to the nearest burrow, signaling the end of a healthy and successful interaction.

2. **Understanding Tiger Salamander interactions with tank mates**

We have already discussed the preference of Tiger salamander for a solitary life. Unless they are sexually stimulated and in the thick of breeding season, the caudates find no particular need for social interaction or companionship. This does not mean that you cannot keep more than one Tiger Salamander in the same vivarium.

Tiger Salamanders are great pets to have around – they are non-interfering, laidback and low-maintenance. It wouldn't be surprising, then, if you felt the desire to bring home more another ambystoma for yourself. It does, however, become important to understand the dynamics that two Tiger Salamanders will share when placed in the same habitat.

How your Tiger Salamander initially reacts to a companion largely depends on the age of both, the caudate you are bringing home and the pet itself. Tiger salamander larvae are more likely to get along than their adult counterparts, as they compete for not more than food. If you are already housing Tiger salamander larvae together, it becomes essential to provide them with a constant supply of nutritious food, as any deficit that they may feel in their feed will change the nature of their relationship with their tank mates.

Harboring underlying cannibalistic tendencies, Tiger salamander larvae will willingly turn on each other for an attempt at survival. Should they feel that their food does not comply with the nutritional requirements needed for their development, they will seek this nourishment from their siblings. Should this phenomenon occur, the cannibalistic nature triggered in your larval pet will manifest into a character trait come adulthood, making it difficult for you to offer it any chance at social interactions. If you already have an adult Tiger Salamander at home, and wish to add a companion to its tank, then not only is the age of the new pet an important factor to consider, but also its physical size, and the size of the tank itself. In a tank that is too small, or just large enough for a solitary Tiger Salamander, the tank mates may become territorial and begin competing with each other for dominance; this may lead to one killing the other, although it is not very common.

When in an aggressive and territorial mood, Tiger Salamanders will size up their competition by factoring their age and size. Generally, it is the older caudate who is also larger and more intimidating. Sometimes, however, if the smaller Tiger salamander is the original occupant of the vivarium, it may become overly defensive of its territory. You should, therefore, consider bringing home a tiger Salamander that close, both in age and size to the one in your tank.

For the most part, if your vivarium is big enough, and your pet has been raised in a secure and content environment, a new companion will be greeted with polite indifference. In the right conditions, the sex of the Tiger Salamanders tank mates has not been observed to make much of a difference. If the caudates do act aggressively, it will be probably be the result of placing two male adult Tiger Salamanders in a shared confined space.

The Tiger Salamanders will generally only interact at mealtimes, preferring to burrow in isolation for the rest of the time. Food being their raison d'etre, the feeding habits that you encourage will determine how aggressive the tank mates become towards each other. If you are the type who feeds the caudates by dangling food from a height, the caudates will gently snip at each other in attempts to be the first to catch it. While not a hostile series of behaviours, this competition may sometimes result in minor cuts and scratches on the toes, sometimes even a missing nail.

It is often considered best to bring home a pair of Tiger Salamander larvae and raise them together, if adopting multiple caudates. With the right conditions, and a generously-sized vivarium of at least a 20-gallon volume should help your Tiger Salamanders exist in perfect harmony.

Chapter Nine: Health Concerns for your Tiger Salamander

Tiger Salamanders have been studied to be one of the few species that have sustained the process of evolution without major or multiple adaptations. This is not a surprising fact, given the caudate ability to withstand life as both aquatic and terrestrial. The resilient nature of the Tiger Salamander's anatomy, coupled with its cautious lifestyle, helps it survive a variety of habitats and well as illnesses. What this means for you as a caregiver, is that your caudate should live out its days in relatively good health, provided you are mindful of its habitat, feeding and cleaning needs. The importance of a hygienic environment becomes especially important for the amphibians, as they spend most of their time in an enclosed space, sharing it with their food as well as fecal matter. If you can maintain a routine by which you constantly clean their premises, your Tiger Salamander should face few, if any, bacterial or viral infections.

This does not mean that your smiling companions have steely demeanour towards illnesses and disease. The Tiger Salamander's skin, its most sensitive organ, is highly reactive to any adverse chemicals, toxins or harmful living bodies such as viral or bacterial colonies. Since the caudate uses the pores on its skin to breathe and receive hydration, any illnesses, infections or internal trauma could be attributed to unhealthy matter absorbed by the dermal tissues.

What makes health concerns a matter of importance in the Tiger Salamander's life is the difficulty to quickly diagnose or isolate what's ailing your pet. As an owner with limited information, you may only have outward symptoms to rely on for an assessment of your pet's health. Since Tiger Salamanders exist in multiple environments simultaneously, however, it is, more often than not, a combination of factors that pushes the caudate health off-balance.

A healthy Tiger Salamander is easily recognizable by his content and restful movement and behaviour patterns. When all its basic necessities, such as a clean habitat, steady live feed and right environmental settings are ensured, the Tiger Salamander will displays such of thriving as:

• Healthy and glossy skin,
• Clear and alert eyes,
• Eager response and behaviours at feeding times
• Refraining from overeating,
• Proper digestion of food, and
• Ideal weight maintenance without tendency towards becoming obese.

As a responsible caregiver, you can address any health concerns that may plague your pet by being watchful of your Tiger Salamander's behaviour, educating yourself on the ailments that may befall it, and locating the nearest exotic pet expert in your area at the earliest.

1. List of Illness and Ailments that May Befall your Tiger Salamander

Ailment/Illness	Physical Symptoms	Possible treatment
Injuries through surroundings debris, tank mates, feed	Scratches, wounds, cuts, abrasions, nips on the outer surface of the skin	Separate from other tank mates in sterile environment and contact exotic pet expert
Rotting of limb	Missing limb or digit, such as leg, foot or toe. Is mostly seen in newly-acquired pets from a vendor. Caused mostly due to infection or injuries sustained from captive housing during trade and sale.	Contact exotic pet vendor to prevent rot from spreading
Sores/Skin	Is mostly seen in newly-	Contact exotic pet vendor for

ulcers	acquired pets from a vendor. Caused mostly due to infection or injuries sustained from captive housing during trade and sale.	right medication. Salt solution may be administered on advice of veterinarian.
Viral/Bacterial/Fungal infections	May appear as fluffy, thread-like white growth or larvae and neotenic, may appear like cloudy white mass on terrestrial caudates. May lso look like bacterial or viral infections.	Contact exotic pet vendor for right medication. Salt solution may be administered on advice of veterinarian. Refrigeration to kill infection may also be prescribed.
Inflamed throat	May be caused due to oral infections or a side effect of digestive disorder such as stomatitis.	Contact exotic pet vendor for right medication.
Clouded eyes	Unclear eyes, sometimes obstructed by a thin white filmy coating. May be incurred due to improper diet, bacterial/viral/fungal infection, toxicity, poor diet or irregular shedding patterns.	Separate from other tankmates in sterile environment and contact exotic pet expert
Irregular shedding/flaking up of dermis	May be incurred due to improper diet, bacterial/viral/fungal infection, toxicity, or poor diet. Is often physical	Separate from other tank mates in sterile environment and contact exotic pet expert

	signal of caudate in distress.	
Intestinal impaction /obstruction	Usually caused in those amphibians such as Tiger salamanders that swallow food whole. Improper breaking down of food may render it an obstacle in the intestines. May also be caused by ingesting small pieces of gravel or debris.	Contact exotic pet expert for possible treatment and surgery, and restructure the substrate, removing all particles that could be ingested.
Metabolic Bone Disease	Onset and prevalence still being studied, but is witnessed to cause deformities to the spine, softer bones, paralysis and even sudden abrupt death in some instances. Is mostly noticeable by sudden loss of appetite in the caudate	Contact exotic pet expert for possible treatment. Incorporate an ideal and higher calcium-phosphorus ratio in feed, along with leveling intake of Vitamins A and D.
Infestation of parasites	Internal or external; include mites, nematodes, anchor worm, etc.	Contact exotic pet vendor for right medication. Salt solution may be administered on advice of veterinarian.
Cloaca-	Collapsing of the walls of	Contact exotic pet vendor for

related ailments	the cloaca, is a dire emergency that needs immediate medical attention	immediate procedure that involves gently easing the walls back and returning the cloaca to position, along with further medication.
Gas bubble disease	Formation of air bubble under the surface of the skin, may be caused due to supersaturation of water with gas (over aeration of water) and cause discomfort to the caudate.	Contact exotic pet vendor for right medication. Salt solution may be administered on advice of veterinarian. Can also be avoided by treating and aging tap water before filling into the tank.
Salamander Plague	Sudden onset caused due to festering of open wound, noticed when wounded area spreads over body, leading to sickness even possible death of Tiger Salamander and mates in the tank.	Separate from other tankmates in sterile environment and contact exotic pet expert for possible treatment of all captive caudates

2. How to tell if your Tiger Salamander is unwell

Most infections that may affect your Tiger Salamander will stem for injuries and wounds that your pet may have incurred in recent times. The Tiger Salamander's skin is extremely thin and sensitive. When faced with a deep cut or open wound, the layers of dermal tissue require time and sterilized conditions to patch up. If left unattended and open in an unhygienic environment, these wounds could easily become a breeding zone for harmful fungi, virus and bacteria.

If you are housing a solitary Tiger Salamander, any wounds or scratches that you notice may have occurred due to injury from its immediate surroundings, such as the corners of the cage or jagged accessories in the tank. Often these minor scrapes will be the result of initial disorientation and panic the caudate feels when introduced to a new environment. Your pet may have also sustained wounds from injuries prior to your bringing it home, and may only become more prominent at later periods.

With a group of two more Tiger Salamanders inhabiting the same space, injuries will stem from minor tussles over space or food. Many of these scratches or nips may even be accidental, unless you have unwittingly housed a cannibal morph among non-cannibals.

However the wounds may have been sustained, it is essential that they are checked and treated at the earliest. Unattended and ignored wounds, especially among animals that inhabit a terrestrial and aquatic zone, can become the perfect breeding hotspot for unwanted micro-organisms. Isolating past injuries as a probable factor of disease is just as important as considering fresh injuries, as many infections show up at a latent stage in Tiger Salamanders, often when it is too late to treat them.

Tiger Salamanders are delicate and complex creatures, requiring care and medical attention that is especially tailored to their anatomies. As a caregiver with just the basic knowledge, you may not always have an accurate idea of your pet's health, or be able to properly diagnose its ailments at a single glance. Indeed, you may also lack the medications needed to effectively treat your pet. To avoid complicating the ambystoma health conditions any further, it is best that you rush it to your exotic pet expert upon noticing the following signs of poor health:

- Open wounds, abrasions or burn-like marks on the curate's skin. Patchy areas in white or red shades are doubly concerning, as these are common indicators of a fungal or bacterial infection;

- Loose, sagging folds of skin covering the caudate body. A healthy Tiger Salamander has skin that is taut, shiny and glossy. If your pet's skin looks like it's folding over itself, displays lesions and wrinkles and feels slippery, it is most likely in physical distress and needs immediate medical attention;

- Appearance of parasites on the skin, particularly on old, untreated injuries;

- Sudden and exaggerated swelling of legs, feet or both;

- Impaired or labored mobility, displayed by difficulty in walking or burrowing; abnormal gait or abnormal/restricted movement of certain or all limbs or digits,

- Poor judgment of balance;

- Dull, listless or cloudy eyes;

- Labored and distressed breathing patterns;

- Swollen, bloated and sensitive-to-touch abdominal area;

- Sudden and rapid weight loss;

- Sudden and constant bouts of diarrhea;

- Refusal of all types of feed with little or no display of eager foraging behavior at feed times;

- Overall display of lethargy for a continued time.

3. Providing Proper Medical Attention for your Tiger Salamander

No matter what ailment may befall your Tiger Salamander, it is important that you not treat it as a simple injury or superficial skin rash that will clear up on its own. Due to the sensitive nature of the Tiger Salamander's skin and its highly reactive tendencies with elements in its surroundings, any open abrasions or minor infections could quickly escalate and become potentially lethal to your pet.
A further obstacle arises in the kind of medicines available to amateur Tiger Salamander enthusiasts or owners for the treatment of their pets. In many cases, infections and ailments that plague your Tiger Salamander may arise from more than one source, and will need a combination of treatments to successfully eliminate. It may be difficult for you to monitor every facet of the Salamander's reaction to the medicine, keep a track of the side effects, and alter doses and medications as needed.

It is for this reason that locating your nearest exotic pet veterinarian becomes essential. In fact, it is best if you track down a reputed and well-trusted expert in your locality before you bring home your first Tiger Salamander. Not only will you have someone to call in case of a health-related emergency with your pet, but most exotic pet experts will also be happy to assist you with all areas of Tiger Salamander care.

Pay close attention to the treatments administered by your exotic pet expert and follow their instructions on medication to the letter. If they ask you to bring your Tiger Salamander in for follow-up procedures and check-ups, do not skip on these. Your pet's medication may need altering and changing after a while, and unneeded administering may cause a relapse or even give rise to new health complications.

If you are housing more than one Tiger Salamander in the same habitat, it is best to quarantine the one that has been infected with a disease. In fact, if your Tiger Salamander sustains so much of an injury, pick it out of the group habitat and place it in a separate quarantine tank. It also becomes important to ensure that the isolated treatment vivarium is sterilized, so as not to agitate the wound further.

Placing your Tiger Salamander in quarantine not only allows your pet to heal and recuperate in a stress-free environment, but also keeps the other pets away from contracting any infections the open wound may bring out. Furthermore, some injuries to the Tiger Salamander may have been caused by the other pets, in a bout of aggression. In these cases, a period of separation gives both the adults time to cool off without causing further harm to either.

Not all illnesses and ailments will affect your Tiger Salamander with the same intensity, and not all will exhibit visible symptoms. In fact, many infections that affect Tiger Salamanders remain visibly latent and hidden for a long time and only manifest as physical symptoms at a critical stage. For these reasons, it is important that you contact your exotic pet expert as soon as your pet appears to display erratic or irregular behaviour.

Do not treat any wound lightly, or resort to treating it yourself, as these may manifest in deadly ways in your pet caudate. A disease that is dangerous to your Tiger salamander's health, called Salamander Plague, is caused when a simple open wound on the caudate skin festers and begins to spread across the body, killing your pet if treated incorrectly.

Finally, as the old adage goes, prevention is better than cure. The best way to ensure that your Tiger salamander receives the best health care is to keep it in the pink of health. Maintain an environment in the vivarium that is clean, sterile and keeps the risk of contracting an illness to a minimum. Along with the supervision of your exotic pet expert, your Tiger Salamander should be able to live a long, healthy, disease-free life.

4. Treating your Tiger Salamander with Salt Solution

If your Tiger Salamander does contract an infection, or experiences discomfort from an ailment, as a caregiver, you will obviously want to give it immediate treatment and relief. The trouble is, unlike other pets, Tiger Salamanders have delicate systems and skin, highly reactive to a number of chemical formulations. This makes their treatment a complicated affair, and calls for the attention of an exotic pet veterinarian.

As a pet Tiger Salamander owner, you may not have a number of medicines at your disposal to quickly alleviate your Tiger Salamanders. You best chance at treatment is often to rush it to the nearest medical centre at the earliest. What you can do from home, however, is provide a simple treatment of salt solution that has been observed to provide relief and antibody removal for the caudates.

After extensive research, several laboratories have themselves used, and then prescribed the use of salt solutions, prepared under rigid guidelines, as an aid to whatever treatment your pet is receiving. So far, carefully concocted salt solution have been found useful in four instances: to extract ectoparasites from the surface of the Tiger Salamanders' skin, to extract fungal growth from the Tiger Salamanders' skin, to extract fungal growth from the surface of Tiger Salamander eggs, and to help alleviate discomfort caused by kidney-related ailments.

The salt used in any treatment related to Tiger Salamander ailments is always non-iodized; any other kind is unacceptable. Ionized forms of salt, such as regular table salt, are manufactured with an added agent that helps keep the salt free-flowing and not clumping up. It is this additive that will agitate, instead of alleviate your pet. When preparing the salt treatments listed below, opt for such types as Kosher salt, sea salt and freshwater aquarium salt.

Treatment for extraction of fungus and ectoparasites

Salt treatments have found to be most effective as an added form of medication for infections caused by the Saprolegnia fungus. Found on the outer surface of the Tiger Salamander's body, the fungi is recognizable by its white or grey fuzzy-looking growth in clumps.

Along with the medications prescribed by your exotic pet expert, you should also indulge your Tiger Salamander in a salt solution exposure, made with water and non-iodized salt. To prepare the solution, combine around 4-6 grams of salt in a liter of water to make a mildly-concentrated solution. For a heavier concentration, you can use between 10-25 grams of salt in a liter of water. It is recommended that you use a lower concentration as far as possible, only making a highly-concentrated dose if prescribed by your exotic pet expert. Even if non-iodized, salt is still harmful for your Tiger Salamander if the caudate is exposed to it for long periods of time.

Ensure that the bowl you place your saline solution in is wide and shallow enough to comfortably place your Tiger Salamander in. It will have to be soaked in till you can successfully remove the fungal growths from its body. Before you handle your Tiger Salamander, ensure that you are wearing medical or latex gloves, with well washed hands just as a precaution.

Now, pick your Tiger Salamander and place it the solution-filled bowl. Allow the amphibian to soak in the water for not more than 30 minutes. While it is submerged, use your hands to pick off and clean away any visible fungal growth. As the soak progresses, you will find it easier to remove any extra growth away. Work quickly and then place your Tiger Salamander back in its vivarium.

If your pet has been hit with a small amount of fungal growth a low concentration with treatment once every 24 hours for around 3 days or so should be adequate. If you are using a high concentrate, reduce the time of exposure as well as the treatments, or lower the concentration so you can prolong the treatment for your Tiger Salamander, if needed.

In addition, should your Tiger Salamander be hit with a fungal growth or infection, it is best to clean and refresh the contents of the vivarium, along with administering a salt solution treatment. A possibly infested habitat will nullify any effects that salt solution has on eliminating fungal growth, causing the caudate undue stress. What may also cause the caudate some stress has to be submerged in the bowl of water against its will.

Not all Tiger Salamanders will allow themselves to be lowered into water against their will; indeed, in some cases you may find them more resistant and stubborn, especially when experiencing kidney troubles. In these cases, instead of placing the animal in water, you can simply place them on a wad of clean salt solution-infused paper towels instead. Simply soak a bunch of paper towels, unleashed, in the solution, and spread them in overlapping layers on a comfortable surface. Carefully place the infused stack on the floor of the vivarium and lay your Tiger Salamander on the paper towel stack, belly-side down. These caudate pores will absorb the effects of salt, causing slow yet guaranteed relief without any fidgeting.

5. Safeguarding your Tiger Salamander against illnesses

If you are the type of pet owner who is considerate and dedicated, then you most likely will already have a caregiving system that is mindful of your Tiger Salamanders needs. In an ideal environment that gives the caudate the right type of food, housing and hygiene conditions, there is little chance that your pet will incur anything more serious than the odd bump or bruise.

Even so, it is always best to take every precaution necessary to safeguard your Tiger Salamander against the possibility of illness and disease. Not only are illnesses very hard on the sensitive amphibian, but several infections sustained by these amphibians also contain carriers such as the salmonella bacteria that could make such species as fish, frogs and even humans, extremely ill. Here are a few ways by which you can ensure the health and well-being of your pet and by extent, your housemates.

1.   A daily cleaning of your Tiger Salamander's cage is not only preferable, it is also essential. As adults, these caudates eat generously and then shed equally generous amounts of excrement that could quickly contaminate an enclosed space. In addition, they also leave behind plenty of uneaten food matter, such as remains from live feed, shells and and exoskeletons of such creatures as crickets.

2.   Any kind of food that could decay and compost, along with all the excrement, should be cleaned out once daily. This, of course, is in addition to the filters

---

that will constantly ensure the water does not become stale too quickly.

3. Since you may not be able to completely handpick all the leftover food particles and the feces, it makes sense to completely overhaul the substrate on a regular basis. Once every two to three months, consider cleaning out your tank entirely and reconstructing the substrate. This will avoid the possibility of any infestations from rotting matter.

4. It is best to avoid putting in such items as small, easy-to swallow stones, twigs, gravel and other ornaments into your vivarium. Since   Tiger Salamanders are curious creatures, they will possibly try to eat objects they do not understand, leading to possible choking hazards and internal injuries, particularly to the stomach and intestines.

5. Tiger   Salamanders best thrive when housed in comfortable temperatures and conditions. They become easily stressed if the climate in their vivarium is either susceptible to erratic changes, or beyond their adaptability range. For this reason, ensure that the temperature in your vivarium never exceeds 75 degrees Fahrenheit.

6. While   Tiger Salamanders may adjust to slightly cooler temperatures, anything higher than the prescribed limit will stress them to an extent   that they may reject food and become morose. If left unchecked, this could become a trigger for various ailments and illnesses.

7. The water you use for the tank – whether as a source for hydration, as a breeding pool, or simply as a place

for Tiger Salamanders to wander in is of utmost importance. Along with being changed at a regular basis, it is essential that the water itself be clean, and more importantly, de-chlorinated.

8. Tap water or filtered water is ideal for your Tiger Salamander's tank. Chemically-treated and chlorine-filled water will release substances   that   will   be absorbed by the Tiger Salamander's spores, leading to adverse effects in most cases, even death.

9. Keep a keen eye on the interaction of your Tiger Salamander, not only   with other caudates if you house them together but also with his environment. The Tiger Salamander may not always show signs of distress, especially if it has been injured. However, watching how   its   surroundings   affect   the amphibian's desire to thrive will help   you   better determine what elements are suitable for your pet, and what agitate or cause it harm.

10. Finally, closely monitor your feeding role as a caregiver, along with the amount of food needed by your Tiger Salamander. While they do not need much to be healthy, Tiger Salamanders have excitable appetites and will not reject food that they find delicious, even if full. It may seem "cute" to watch your caudate scurry about   foraging his food, and then gobble it up with a grin, but enabling it too far may lead to an overly-chubby amphibian. The odd extra work, thrown in for both, the pet's delight as well as yours, is fine. A daily habit of over-feeding your pet will result in a Tiger Salamander with obesity and other health-related issues.

Chapter Nine: Breeding Tiger Salamanders for a Profit

Tiger Salamanders make for perfect long-term companions – they take up little space, need virtually no attention, and are content to spend their days without any social interaction. The seemingly ideal lifestyle they exhibit may tempt you to breed some of these specimen for your own. As a caregiver, ushering your pet through the stages of sexual maturity may feel almost like a parental responsibility. Or you may want to start raising some of these caudates for a profit, having successfully taken care of your own pet. Understand, however, that breeding Tiger Salamanders is a challenging undertaking.

In their natural habitat, the usually solitary Tiger Salamanders only look for a companion when the breeding season arrives. In addition, they have observed, over the years, to have a difficulty breeding when in captivity. There have been several attempts, both small and large-scale, to extend the lineage of several existing specimen in captivity – with little success. Methods such as mimicking the Tiger Salamander's natural surroundings have managed to stimulate breeding behaviours in some caudates, but there is still no breeding process that can guarantee you success.

If you must, however, take the risk and attempt to breed the caudates, whether for personal use or profit, this chapter will guide you through the process, which consists of three stages – encouraging the caudates to go into estivation, stimulating breeding patterns after the estivation period, and getting the Tiger Salamander to deposit a fertilized egg sack. This chapter will also guide you through the right way to provide care for the Tiger Salamander eggs and subsequent hatched larvae – should you succeed in your attempts.

1.   Stimulating a Breeding Environment for the Tiger Salamanders

If you have made up your mind to give breeding your Tiger Salamanders in captivity a try, you will have to first take the time to set up a breeding zone for them. Ideally, a breeding pond that best mimics their natural surroundings is what you should aim for. Bear in mind, however, that setting up a breeding zone for your caudates is a time-consuming affair and will need you to be mindful of the pets' needs at every stage.

One of the first factors that will influence the success rate of your breeding attempt is the temperature and climate of the area you reside in. Tiger Salamanders have been studied to breed generously and even through the non-breeding seasons in those regions with warmer climates. Temperatures that mimic the arrival of spring may be able to trigger breeding patterns in the caudates and encourage them to mate.

Even if the temperatures around you are favorable enough for breeding, this is the just the first in a long list of factors, all of which must work in harmony. Tiger Salamanders commence their breeding behaviors at the first sign of warm climate, but only after a period of shutting down and cooling off for a certain amount of time. This process of estivation is essential for the Tiger Salamanders' reproductive patterns to kick into gear, and will have to be undertaken for a higher success rate.

You should ideally allow your Salamanders to go into estivation during the winter months, when all rooms in your house will be cooler. It is also important that the area of estivation be dark to encourage faster shutting down of the caudates' systems. Choose a quiet, cool and dark area, away from the hustle and bustle of your daily routines, at a temperature ranging between 60 to 65 degrees Fahrenheit. You will not need to prepare a separate estivation environment for the Tiger Salamanders; if designed correctly, your vivarium should be the perfect hibernation zone.

The next stage in the estivation process is to withdraw food from the Tiger Salamanders. Ensure that your pets have been well-fed for at least a couple of months before they shut down. A steady diet of nutrient-rich live feed should ensure that they will sleep through the next month or two in comfort. Once you have placed them in the hibernation room, stop feeding them until the time for them to emerge for breeding arrives. Also try to ensure that there isn't any live food debris left in their tank, such as tiny worms or bugs. These may encourage foraging behaviours in the Salamander, instead of lulling them into hibernation.

Allow your Tiger Salamanders to remain in this estivation state for at least a month, two months at the most. Do not disturb their environment during this time, except to check up on them every so often. This estivation phase is also the perfect amount of time you need to set up their breeding habitat. And in some cases, the perfect amount of time for you to consider whether you want to carry through with the rest your plan.

The need to construct a separate breeding zone for the caudates largely depends on the size and design of their current vivarium. If your tank is larger than the 20-gallon requirement for a pair of Tiger Salamander adults, it is certainly large enough to comfortably allow the pair to undergo the rituals of mating. What is equally important, however, is the availability of an abundant aquatic source for the deposition of first, spermatozoa, and then, the fertilized egg sack.

If you incorporated an aquatic space, such as a makeshift pool or an artificial pond at the time of setting up your vivarium, this could serve as the ideal breeding pond for the caudates. In fact, the comfort and familiarity of the space may even help stimulate their breeding patterns early. In case your tank has been set up as a terrestrial zone, however, you may need to either add a small water body to the tank, or construct a separate breeding pond for the caudates.

It is the rise in temperatures that first signals the end of the estivation period for the Tiger Salamanders. If you are setting up your breeding pond externally, therefore, consider such spots as your backyard or maybe a cooler section of a greenhouse or indoor garden, if you have one. Once this breeding spot has been successfully set up, you can begin ushering your pets out of hibernation and into the breeding phase.

Towards the later part of the Tiger Salamanders' estivation, you will have to prepare them for this increase in temperature. Understand that you cannot abruptly pick them out of a cool spot and place them in a breeding-friendly habitat over the course of a day. The sudden shift in temperatures may, far from stimulating breeding patterns, actually shock and shut down any possible chances for mating. Instead, you will, once again, mimic the rising patterns of temperature by turning up the heat at a gradual rate.

Try to increase the heat by about a degree every two days, slow enough to nudge, instead of force them out of estivation. Continue this for about a week or two, until you have given those around two days to adjust to the temperature of the intended breeding pond, be it the tank or an external space. By this time, they should have begun to emerge from their burrows, enabled by the heat.

If your breeding pond is housed within the vivarium, it is here that the Tiger Salamanders should move to deposit their spermatozoa and subsequent egg sack. If the breeding pond is outside the house, gently move the tank to the intended spot. You can do this just before they emerge from their burrows in the quiet hours of the night, with a cloth covering the tank to preserve the Tiger Salamanders' privacy. Either leave the cover open, or place them in the breeding zone right after they burrow themselves out.

As encouraging as the warm temperatures may be, we have learned now that Tiger Salamanders become stimulated not just by the arrival of spring, but specifically after the first rains or thundershowers. While the specific reasons for this phenomenon are still being researched, what we do know is that giving your pets a taste of "first rains", whether natural or artificially rendered, may help activate their breeding patterns.

Depending on the place you live, you could choose from one of two popular methods adopted by those who have successfully bred these picky caudates. Those breeders who live in warmer climates with generous rainfall at springtime, have simply created outdoor breeding ones for their caudates, allowing them to share in the natural changes in weather and soak in the early showers for themselves. While not always successful, this is the closest you can come to mimicking the natural breeding requisites for your pets.

If you'd like to leave little to the hands of fate, and prefer to take matters into your own hands, however, you can go the way of other successful breeders, who created rain chambers for their pets. With the help of various gardening watering equipment, such as pumps and misters set at particular heights and angles, you can re-create the idea of a gentle shower, or a steady smattering of raindrops. The additional advantage of setting up sprinklers, pumps and misters to provide "rains" is that you can control the timings of your showers, and ensure that the caudates receive "rainfall" each time.

Provided the above steps all go as planned, your Tiger Salamander pets should be stimulated enough and ready to mate with each other. To successfully do so, the adult male will need a large flat piece of submerged debris to deposit his spermatozoa upon. You can provide such a surface by placing such items as small, road logs, twigs and sticks at regular intervals at the bottom. Be mindful that you do not overcrowd the bottom or leave sharp debris that may injure the Tiger Salamanders. Leaf surfaces are also used as spermatozoa drop-zones, so any old leafy twigs you can find will be helpful.

When the adult male Tiger Salamander has done his part, the female adult should enter the water and pick up the spermatozoa to deposit within her. Because she too, has to travel to the same spot, ensure that bottom is spacious and comfortable enough to allow her to place the sperm sacs at her cloaca for entrance. After a period about 24 to 48 hours, the female should then find a spot within the same pond to deposit the fertilized egg sack.

Among her top choices will be broad twigs and sticks, possibly even branches with leaves. As you will need to personally move the object that she lays her eggs on, ensure that you pick those debris that are most conveniently-suited to both, the adult breeding pair and to you.

2.   Caring for the Tiger Salamander Eggs

If you have managed to stimulate the breeding behaviors among your adult Tiger Salamanders and convinced them to formulate a fertilized egg sack, then the hardest part of your endeavor is now behind you. Indeed, caring for the Tiger Salamander eggs, and the larvae that will hatch from them, is a relative breeze compared to the efforts put into getting your pets to mate.

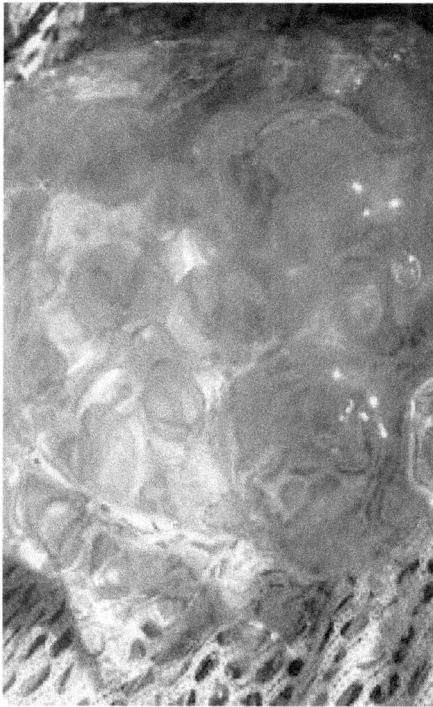

While your female adult Tiger Salamander is fertilizing the spermatozoa within her and looking for a spot on which to deposit the egg pouch, you will want to prepare a separate holding tank for the eggs she hatches. Whether the breeding pond be within the vivarium or in an external zone, you do not want to house the eggs and adults together, as a measure against any unwanted damage to the former.

For the egg enclosure, all you really need to do by way of preparation is find a suitable tank for the hatching process and fill it with water. A simple tank with a volume of about 10 gallons has been found to serve its purpose with ease. The only prerequisite for the water you fill into the tank is that it should be de-chlorinated. High levels of chlorine content in the water may damage the eggs. Fill the tank about halfway, and your preparation is complete.

The unhatched eggs have no requirements for a specific type of substrate or environment. Furthermore, the eggs are perfectly content at being housed at untreated water, so you do need to worry about investing in additional filtering equipment and apparatus. As long as they are submerged in water under the right temperature and left undisturbed, they should hatch without any problems.

As mentioned, the right temperature window is crucial for the survival and hatching of your Tiger Salamander eggs. The ideal temperature bracket for successful gestation and hatching lies between 65 and 75 degrees Fahrenheit. In most cases, you should be able to achieve this by housing your tank in a warm room and leaving the water to settle at room temperature.

If you live in a colder area, and need to regulate the temperature manually, ensure that you maintain one that falls safely between these brackets, even after slight changes in either direction. It has been observed in nature that Tiger Salamander eggs deposited in warmer water tend to hatch at a faster rate. Mimicking these natural phenomena, your egg pouch too, will most likely thrive in a warmer temperature, with a tendency hatch sooner. Be very careful, however: if your water is too cold, you may have caused probable harm to the eggs, but water that is too hot will definitely cause irreparable damage to the eggs.

Once your egg enclosure is ready and the female adult Tiger Salamander has deposited the eggs, all you have to do is pick up the debris with the eggs and transfer them into their designated tank. This is a delicate process that requires great care and attention on your part. It is essential that you make the egg transfer without disturbing the eggs themselves in any way. The contents of this fertilized matter are highly delicate and will become unyielding at the slightest provocation.

To safely pick up the egg capsule, simply pick up the twig or branch that the female has laid the eggs on, but do so very gently. If the branch is small enough to be carried without moving the eggs or encountering any obstacles such as the edges of the tank, go ahead and lift it up. If the piece of debris is too big, however, or located in an external breeding pond, you will then need to clip away the section holding the eggs away from the larger debris.

To do so, use a small pair of clippers or scissors and delicately make the snip, without disturbing the eggs. It is for purposes of easy handling and transferring that debris such as broad and flat twigs, branches and leaves are suggested in an artificial breeding pond. Leaves attached to branches especially make for ideal depositing as well as transferring carriers. Then, carry the debris over to the hatching tank, keeping your other hand below for support. If you can keep the tank close to the breeding pond at the time of transfer, it would be perfect.

If your egg pouch is too crowded together on a small surface (highly unlikely as females will look for large and broad surfaces), cut away a larger part to avoid any of the eggs moving or falling in the transfer. If the process of transferring seems overly cautious, it is because Tiger Salamander eggs demand a rigidly caring hand through every phase of the handling. Do not try and take shortcuts such as picking the eggs up with your fingers and dropping them into the enclosure. You will definitely rupture the contents of the eggs this way, and undo all your patience and hard work.

Once the transfer has been completed, all you have to do is wait for the eggs to hatch. Based on the temperatures that you have set up in your tank, the Tiger Salamander eggs should take about two to three weeks to hatch. The hatching time, however, has known to vary a lot, and is mostly reliant on the temperature of the water, so be prepared for them to hatch a little earlier, or even much later.

3.   Caring for the Tiger Salamander larvae

The three weeks or so between the time of transferring the fertilized eggs and the hatching is your time of reprieve and preparation for the final stage of the breeding endeavor: raising the hatched larvae. While not as calculated and tricky a procedure as the first phase of estivating the adult Tiger Salamanders, this final part still involves more work and possible financial investment than the relatively effortless hatching phase.

While your Tiger Salamander eggs are hatching, take the time to prepare a separate enclosure for your resultant Tiger Salamander larvae. A newly hatched group of Tiger salamander larvae are a little-sized bunch, and can be comfortably housed in a tank as small as one with a volume of five gallons. However, it is important to understand that, should you choose to house them in a small tank at the beginning, you will need to upgrade them every few weeks to bigger tanks as the larvae will develop into mature-sized adults at a rapid rate, usually within a couple of months.

To prepare the tank, all you need is to do initially is fill the tank with water the same temperature as the one used for hatching the eggs, around 65 to 75 degrees Fahrenheit. A comfortable driving environment is created by this temperature bracket, allowing your Tiger Salamander larvae to develop at a steady rate. Filtering devices are not needed for the water when your Tiger Salamander larvae are freshly hatched. They do not create enough waste as infants to dirty the water quickly, and furthermore, are tiny and delicate enough that they may be sucked in by the whir of the filter. A simple changing of the used water for fresh and clean water every alternate day for the first few weeks will suffice.

During this time, you will also need to start preparing food acceptable for your Tiger Salamander larvae. Live feed items, such as earthworms and red worms are the perfect starter food for the larvae. You will, however, need to cut up the food before you feed it to the larvae, as their mouths and systems are too delicate to handle large morsels so quickly.

Other soft, delicate aquatic invertebrates, such as chopped shrimp may also be given infrequently. For the right foods, refer to the checklist of acceptable foods in the chapter on feeding your Tiger Salamanders. Since the food portions will be small and the Tiger Salamander larvae cannot be exposed to your bare skin, use a pair of tweezers or forceps (sterilized, first) to pick the chopped food up and hold in the tank for the larvae to pluck away.

It is important, at this juncture, to remind you of the voracious appetites your Tiger Salamander larvae will have. In the early stages of their life, and fast approaching metamorphosis, Tiger Salamander larvae spend much of their early days feeding on bait that will enhance their development. In fact, so focused are they on procuring food, that any shortage they may feel they face in terms of frequency of feed or nutritional requirements, will be quickly corrected by turning cannibalistic. This is a fate you want to completely avoid.

Tiger Salamander larvae who turn cannibalistic may develop faster and grow to be larger than others, this is true. They will, however, and then need to be completely isolated from the rest of the group, for the survival of all. It behoves us to remind you that cannibal Tiger Salamander larvae will most definitely grow into cannibal adults, thus endangering the future of your other pets, should they be housed together.

Therefore, it is essential that you not only provide the right type of food at regular intervals of around two times a day for your larvae, but also that you stay alert and watchful of their behaviour. Sometimes, despite your best efforts, their increasing appetites may mean that they turn cannibalistic anyway. As soon as they exhibit signs of attacking their siblings, transfer them into separate enclosures, tanks small enough to contain them till adulthood. In fact, you may have to separate your Tiger Salamander larvae into smaller groups in any case, as they eventually get too big to be housed together.

As they grow, the Tiger Salamander larvae will also begin to create more waste than before. This will mean that after the first two or three weeks, you will need to install a simple filter into the tank to clean away waste. The best time to do this once your larvae have grown too big to fit through the tiny spaces of the filter, and are big enough not to be drawn in by the tiny current of water the filter generates. Successful Tiger Salamander breeders have found that simple biological canister filters work best for the Tiger Salamander larvae, so consider investing in one (or more) for your large-holding tanks.

Provided the next two to three months with your Tiger Salamander larvae go well, you should have them metamorphose into beautiful adults in a smooth motion. You will notice that the feathery extensions on their heads, used as gills for breathing, would have disappeared and become replaced by land breathing internal organs and a striking coat. If certain Tiger Salamanders exhibit signs of neoteny, you will then have to take care of them in an aquatic environment. Once the metamorphosis is complete, you are ready to house them in an adult vivarium and care for them from there on.

4.   Understanding the Risks of Tiger Salamander breeding in captivity

If you have bred a successful batch of Tiger Salamander larvae in captivity, please take a moment to truly appreciate and celebrate your hard work up until this point. It is considered among the most challenging tasks to stimulate their breeding patterns in an artificial environment; that you have done so is a testament to your commitment. However, before you undertake this arduous task, it is wise to consider the amount of factors that surround the stimulation and subsequent care for Tiger Salamanders during each phase of the breeding endeavour.

To begin with, there are few accounts of successful Tiger Salamander breeding attempts, especially when conducted on a large scale. Several of the requisites are tricky to imitate on a large scale, especially if you want to breed Tiger Salamanders for a profit. Being ambystomatidae, Tiger Salamanders are loyal to their place of birth and often try to return to this spot to breed. You will have to bring them home at a very young age – possibly even as eggs – and have them recognize your enclosure as their home for any signs of success.

If you are able to arouse feelings of breeding in them, it then becomes your responsibility to let them undergo estivation, and then prepare their bodies for the early heat and rains of the springtime. If not naturally available, this simulated environment is difficult, time-consuming and even expensive to create. Once created, you will have to keep a watchful eye on the proceedings, and regulate such factors as temperature – without disturbing the natural patterns of the caudates themselves.

The trickiest part arrives when the estivation period has ended and the Tiger salamanders are now expected to commence mating rituals. A number of things may not go according to plan here – the estivation period may have been inadequate or deficient in some way. There may not be enough or consistent rains for the Tiger Salamanders to begin breeding behaviours, or the artificially stimulated showers may not work as planned. The breeding pond may be rejected by the adult Tiger Salamanders, or they may even reject each other as potential mates. The success of this phase, despite all your hard work, is entirely dependent on the will of the Tiger Salamanders.

Furthermore, should you be able to successfully procure Tiger Salamander eggs, it then adds to your responsibility – and expenses – to provide a housing that allows them to develop through each stage of growth. This will include buying a number of tanks, changing water constantly, doubling up on splitting feeding and cleaning duties between the adults and babies and installing new filtering devices, to name a few. The larvae may also become cannibalistic, rendering your attempts at breathing the young ones futile.

There is then the future problem of long-term care for the hatchlings. If successfully raised to their adult stage, you will have dozens of Tiger Salamanders to care for. You can choose to sell them to interested individuals, or choose to sell them to a local reputed vendor, but these practices will have to be permitted and legal within your residence. Indeed, the entire process of breeding your adults, whether for personal use or profit, is futile without legal permits from the concerned authorities.

On a personal note, this endeavour, rewarding as it may be, will consume a large part of your free time, and require dedication, as well as patience on your part. Every phase of the breeding process will also affect the people you live with, be it friends or family, making it essential that they are cooperative of your plans. When you do decide to breed your Tiger Salamanders, take the time to consider the circumstances surrounding their breeding, and the amount of factors you leave to chance – it will help you make a decision that works out for you.

Resources

- http://www.caudata.org/cc/articles/tiger_sal_101.shtml
- http://www.reptilesncritters.com/care-guide-tiger-salamander.php
- http://www.reptilesmagazine.com/Care-Sheets/Frogs-Amphibians/Tiger-Salamander-Care-Sheet/
- http://www.peteducation.com/article.cfm?c=17+1848&aid=2953
- http://www3.northern.edu/natsource/AMPHIB1/Salama1.htm
- https://en.wikipedia.org/wiki/Tiger_salamander#As_pets
- http://www.savethesalamanders.com/why-salamanders-matter.html
- http://animals.mom.me/tiger-salamanders-habitats-1386.html
- http://www.caudata.org/cc/species/Ambystoma/A_tigrinum.shtml
- http://www.theamphibian.co.uk/tiger_salamander_care_sheet.htm
- http://www.petplace.com/article/reptiles/general/reptile-profiles/choosing-a-tiger-salamander
- http://exoticpets.about.com/cs/salamanders/a/tigersalamander.htm
- http://www.wikihow.com/Take-Care-of-Tiger-Salamanders
- http://small-pets.lovetoknow.com/reptiles-amphibians/tiger-salamander-care

Resources

- https://en.wikipedia.org/wiki/Barred_tiger_sala
  mander
- http://www.petco.com/caresheets/amphibians/sa
  lamander_tiger.pdf
- http://www.ecohealthypets.com/browse_animals
  /amphibians/6-tiger_salamander
- http://www.amphibiancare.com/frogs/caresheets
  /tigersalamander.html
- http://www.axolotl.org/tiger_salamander.htm
- http://www.env.gov.bc.ca/okanagan/esd/atlas/sp
  ecies/tiger_salamander.html
- http://asalamanderstory.tumblr.com/page/2
- http://www.caudata.org/cc/articles/foods.shtml
- http://small-pets.lovetoknow.com/reptiles-
  amphibians/salamanders-diet
- http://www.petco.com/assets/caresheets/amphib
  ians/salamanders-and-newts.pdf
- http://www.caudata.org/cc/articles/illness.shtml
- http://www.caudata.org/cc/articles/salt.shtml

www.ingramcontent.com/pod-product-compliance
Lightning Source LLC
Chambersburg PA
CBHW072020040426

42447CB00009B/1670